We Don't Do God

We Don't Do God

John Burton

Eileen McCabe

continuum

Continuum
The Tower Building, 11 York Road, London SE1 7NX
80 Maiden Lane, Suite 704, New York, NY 10038

www.continuumbooks.com

First published 2009

British Library Cataloguing-in-Publication Data
A catalogue record for this book is available from the British Library.

ISBN 978-184706-352-6

Typeset by Kenneth Burnley, Wirral, Cheshire
Printed and bound by the MPG Books Group

Contents

Author's Note

This is not an attempt to record the detail of Tony Blair's premiership and New Labour. What we have endeavoured to do is to explore those policies that illustrate the impact of Blair's Christian beliefs on domestic and foreign policy.

If we paint a positive picture of the former Prime Minister, this reflects the close working relationship between Blair and co-author, John Burton, who was Blair's mentor and agent for 25 years. However, the book also strives to tell the story in such a way that allows readers to make up their own minds about the Blair years. For this reason, the narrative stands alone from Burton's italicized contributions.

Eileen McCabe
January 2009

St John's College, Oxford, 1972–5

The vaulted passage opposite the main gate of St John's College leads under the President's Lodging into Canterbury Quad. On the east and west sides stand magnificent Tuscan arcades. The college library sits on the south side while the Laudian Library stretches 'proud and promising' above the eastern colonnade. Amidst the architectural splendour, a room off the south spur of the Quad provides a lofty meeting place for a band of long-haired undergraduates eager to pool their raw thoughts.

Questions range from reform and revolution to the relationship between theology and politics, from the concept of communitarian politics to the redistribution of wealth. Their host is a slender, upright older man, a hard-hitting bronzed Australian. As he greets the young acolytes, observers might be forgiven for thinking that the lure of free cigarettes, wine and coffee brings the motley group together, but the main attraction is Peter Thomson, a charismatic character oozing charm and enthusiasm and a passion for tub-thumping discussion.

Given a certain level of undergraduate posturing, the standard of debate is rather more profound than their youth might suggest. Variations on socio-religious themes are tortuously dissected. 'Christianity must have a practical component otherwise religion has no meaning.' 'Values without politics is ineffective.' 'The equal worth of people and the right to be treated with respect and consideration is fundamental.' 'Individual responsibilities and the obligations owed to one another.' Topics the average student would address only if tutors held pistols to their heads.

By midnight, empty cigarette packets lie alongside smelly ashtrays, the coffee has long since gone cold, but the young students continue to debate the prospect of entwining faith and politics (an idea that writers of the New Testament rejected two millennia ago).

The guest list varies from session to session but stalwarts of Peter Thomson's must-go-to soirées include Geoff Gallop, a fellow Australian, Rhodes Scholar and a member of the International Marxist Group who was to become Premier of Western Australia; Olara Otunna, a Ugandan refugee and an evangelical Christian, a future United Nations Special Representative for Children; a bunch of assorted newspaper and television journalists; and Tony Blair, neither particularly political nor religious but strangely drawn to Thomson's brand of Christian socialism and who would become one of the most controversial British prime ministers in recent times.

Given his future place on the world stage, Blair was the least political of the group, but Thomson's influence would change all that. Blair said later that he found him 'spell-binding', describing him as 'one of the most inspiring, honest and decent people I have ever met in my life. There's nothing soft about him. He's tough, he's courageous. His Christianity is instructive.'[1]

Thomson, who has said little over the years about his friendship with Blair, recalled:

I was an old retard who had arrived here from Australia, trying to become respectable. He was young, full of life, a person who had this *joie de vivre*. He was into life. He'd a keen intellect and a sense of compassion for other people. And we had these marvellous discussions that would go on for hours.[2]

Thomson was one of a handful of people who inspired and helped shape Blair's political thinking and turned an aimless, part-time rock performer into a serious young man who, in time, would fuse his Christianity and left-of-centre politics into a reasonable and relevant explanation of life. Yet no one who knew Blair at Oxford – neither tutors nor contemporaries – marked him out as a future leader.

Introduction

For the man who governed Britain for ten years, the magic moment – albeit a bizarre moment – came in March 2007 during the BBC's fundraising programme, *Comic Relief*, just months before his resignation.

Ensconced in the grandeur of his Downing Street office with work experience schoolgirl Lauren (alias Catherine Tate), Tony Blair feigns increasing irritation at her 'Am I bovvered' bluster. Cameras pan from Prime Minister to ASBO girl and back to Prime Minister struggling to stay calm as she rants about everything from trainers to Top Shop. The camera moves in for the final close-up as Blair's voice, in perfect Laurenesque pitch, snaps, 'Face? Bovvered?'

Can you imagine any other politician attempting the same sketch and pulling it off? Blair, the actor–politician, could put to one side the constraints of prime ministerial office at the click of a producer's fingers and walk straight into a television classic. It was a brilliant off-the-leash moment for the man who was about to leave the political stage, liberated from the burden of office and the prospect of fighting a fourth election campaign. For the duration of the sketch, it was almost possible to forget the issues that were plunging the Labour Party into despair: the 'cash for honours' investigation, Iraq, the pensions scandal, public sector reform, the EU constitution.

'Am I bovvered? Face? Bovvered?' Was he bothered about the avalanche of crises that threatened to destroy his legacy in those final months at Number 10? Was he bothered at his premiership cut short in the aftermath of a Gordon Brown-backed abortive coup in September 2006? Was he bothered about the febrile tread of the law as it raked through Downing Street files and computers during the 'cash for honours' affair?

Certainly his exit route was never going to be strewn with roses from a grateful nation, but even Blair could never have predicted the avalanche of ridicule and odium that was to spew from those whose only pleasure was 'building mausoleums for enemies'. Those close to him knew the full extent of the beleaguered Prime Minister's wrath at being entangled in such an unimaginable trap. In a radio interview in February 2007 he refused to bow to the ever-mounting pressure. 'I'm not going to beg for my character in front of anyone. People can make up their own mind about me, according to what they think of me, but I know what type of person I am.'[1]

It was a desolate time for the man who, in the first years of his premiership, had experienced unprecedented popularity. During these dark, pre-resignation days, he needed all the friendly support he could muster. John Burton, Blair's agent for almost 25 years, was one of a handful of people close to the Prime Minister as one of the longest parliamentary goodbyes in history was played out. During Blair's visits to his Sedgefield constituency, the two men discussed the issues surrounding his resignation as his authority plummeted with every passing day. It was ironic that as his status as a world leader peaked, when finally he had a clear idea of a public service reform agenda, the Prime Minister's personal rating in the polls slumped, much to the delight of his embittered Chancellor.

John Burton: *Sadness and despair is how I would sum up my feelings at the time. We had achieved so much in ten years, and conspiracy after conspiracy was undermining all that good work. You can criticize Tony's decisions and question his thinking but as soon as his integrity was savaged, well . . . that really hurt. Tony's religion and politics are bound together and although people might question this or that or say he got it wrong, he was genuinely shocked if they questioned his morality because there was never a dividing line between his politics and Christianity – not down on your knees and praying religion but faith in action, finding a way of making life better for people, of buffeting a secular society that dominated life in Britain. He believed it was time to nudge it in the other direction.*

While he was at Number 10, Tony was virtually gagged on the whole question of religion. Alastair (Campbell) was convinced it would get him into trouble with the voters. But Tony's Christian faith is part of him, down to his cotton socks. How can you understand his thinking on any front if you don't understand his core beliefs? He believed strongly, although he couldn't say it at the time, that intervention in Kosovo, Sierra Leone – Iraq too – was all part of the Christian battle; good should triumph over evil, making lives better, not necessarily because of religion itself but because of shared universal values that could be a guide in a troubled world going through the most difficult times.

In his final months at Number 10, Blair was living in parallel worlds: in public, the beleaguered Prime Minister hounded by the press and his own party, while in private, robust and defiant, confident of his place in history. Moreover, political tensions within the Party, and disillusion generally in the country, made it difficult to assess the impact of Blair's ten-year premiership. In truth, the man who had achieved two landslide victories plus a third with a respectable majority, should have been able to effect radical public sector reform, yet by his own admission he failed to take advantage of the opportunity that his massive majorities and unique popularity presented. That said, throwing brickbats at the government exonerated those critics who launched periodic attacks on Blair's God in whose name he sought power.

However history may judge the Blair years, it is important to step back and examine the damaging divisions that existed in the early 1980s within the Labour Party which was unelectable as it clung to a dog-eared agenda: nationalization, the closed shop, high spend/low taxation policies, unwilling to listen to the growing aspirations of the Party's traditional supporters. Blair changed the Party and the face of British politics for ever as he fought for and secured the centre ground. But were golden opportunities squandered? Did he fail to stand up to the tough morality demanded by his Christian faith? Did he modify his religious beliefs during his ten-year premiership? How did the easy relationship with his Maker impact on decision-making? Did high office turn him into a raging authoritarian (especially after 9/11), intransigent and less willing to listen to the views of others?

Where do you begin? Do you start with Blair's historic Clause IV moment, the sacred century-old dogma that many said could never be revoked? Or securing peace in Northern Ireland? Or do you start with Blair's leftist utterances on the redistribution of wealth and attacks on poverty that may be more difficult to identify? For many people, the starting point will continue to be his crusade against international terrorism and interventionist ambitions that he hoped would achieve global justice and tolerance and freedom.

The tidy-minded might say his lofty ambitions were never going to be achieved, that rhetoric was a poor substitute for substance, and that his first term in office was squandered despite it being wrapped in the golden glow of a landslide victory, a strong economy and unprecedented personal ratings. But despite the criticism, how do you judge the man who always said he believed 100 per cent in what he was doing, whether it was reaching out to the Tory hinterland where no other Labour leader dared go, or ordering troops into combat, bamboozling his opponents or dividing his own party.

While Blair was in power, Burton said little about the moral commitment and faith that lay behind much of the Prime Minister's thinking. Advisers insisted it was a no-win topic; non-believers were disinterested and believers would question his motives for going public. Following an interview with Matthew d'Ancona in the *Sunday Telegraph* in

1996, Blair said afterwards: 'I shouldn't have done it and I won't do it again.' But as time puts distance between Blair and his premiership, Burton admits that whether it was raising standards in schools or intervening in Iraq, Blair's moral and religious code was the key driving force during his time at Number 10; the Prime Minister who preached that society could not live in a moral vacuum and Christian values should become more, not less, relevant.

Given their different backgrounds, the Blair–Burton partnership might seem unlikely. Blair was the product of an affluent, middle-class Tory background, public school and Oxford educated, and in 1976 he secured a pupillage at Derry Irvine's prestigious Chambers. His father, Leo, was a lifelong atheist and an active member of the Conservative Party until a stroke destroyed his dream of becoming a Tory MP. It was left to Hazel Blair to take the children to church, although there is little evidence that religion held any particular appeal to the boy Blair.

Burton's background was firmly rooted in the North East and the Church. John attended local schools before completing a teacher training course at St Bede's College in Durham. His father, Donald, also a teacher, was a Labour councillor and Burton followed in his father's footsteps as teacher, local politician and committed Christian; he took over from his father as secretary to the local church council and is a member of the church council serving on the Deanery and Diocesan Synods. As a young man, Burton considered going into the Church but decided he could make a greater contribution to the community through the local political system (although he was to stray into the highest echelons of government).

Observers have described the Blair–Burton relationship as more father–son than political allies. (Burton, with a twinkle in his eye, respectfully suggests that the age differential is not so great.) Certainly their shared political and Christian beliefs have been the cornerstone of their friendship and political ambition.

Peter Mandelson had this to say:

What John gave to Tony was a hinterland, a knowledge in depth, a feel, an experience, a reach into the Labour Party, its history, its soul, its human make-up. Via John, Tony was able to acquire through his own instinctive grasp and understanding of situations, a knowledge of what made people tick.[2]

Burton's place in Blair's political life has been pivotal. Indeed it is doubtful whether he would have become Prime Minister without his Sedgefield mentor, a debt Blair readily acknowledges: 'I would say in my own personal development, he was one of the four or five most influential people in my life.'[3]

Perhaps it is no coincidence that the 'four or five most influential people in my life' had one thing in common, the same sense of purpose to take a living, breathing religion and with it help create a more tolerant, equitable society. 'Your religious beliefs aren't something that you shut away from the world but something that means you have to go out and act', said Blair.

No one can accuse Tony Blair of lack of action. Against the howling protests of the Party, it led him to revoke Clause IV, to seek and secure an historic breakthrough in Northern Ireland and to reform, or at least halt, the decline of public services. It also led him to Kosovo and Sierra Leone and Iraq.

How was his foreign policy coloured by his religious beliefs? Did his Christian conscience demand that he trample on tyranny, whether it was Serbia's Slobodan Milosevic or Iraq's Saddam Hussein? Did he ever pause to assess his predilection for liberal interventionism against St Augustine's 'just-war' teachings? (In the run-up to the Iraq war, Blair avoided questions that implied his judgement was based on religious beliefs.)

Since Blair stood down as Prime Minister, he has taken every opportunity to explain how his religious and political beliefs are intertwined. No longer shackled by the Downing Street machine, he has paraded his faith in churches and conference halls along with a multi-faith dialogue and a conviction that all world religions, correctly adhered to, will lead to God.

To understand the Blair premiership, then, we need to understand his faith. To understand his faith, we need to trace his journey to Number 10 in the company of a handful of Christian centre-left mentors, each contributing to a remarkable career that owed much to liberal Christian thinking that, nevertheless, led him into the waiting arms of the Roman Catholic Church just six months after leaving office.

PART I

CHAPTER 1

Oxford to Sedgefield

The Christian stress on community, on man's relationship, not only with God but also with his fellow man, is the essential reason why I am on the left rather than the right.[1]

For aspiring Members of Parliament, the road to Westminster is signposted with checklists of prescribed policies dictated by decades of deep-rooted, hot-blooded tradition. Tony Blair's journey differed. Blair had no such checklist other than a set of values firmly rooted in his Christian faith. Moreover, unlike other British prime ministers – Harold Wilson, Margaret Thatcher, Gordon Brown, who all showed a keen interest in politics from an early age, propping up student political gatherings and delivering impassioned pleas to party conferences – Blair was a late starter who happened to have the good fortune to meet a number of key people at key times in key positions.

Fate seemed to take a hand in pointing the young Blair in the direction of those of a certain disposition whose politics and Christian beliefs dovetailed in what might be described as the union of the individual and the community. In assessing Blair's early journey, this mixed bunch of influential and intellectual champions was critical in moulding the views of the future Prime Minister over a period of 11 years – from 1972 and his time at Oxford to his arrival on John Burton's doorstep in 1983.

When he left school in 1971, Blair had no clear idea what he wanted to do with his life, and there was certainly no evidence of a political leader in the making. If he had any ambition, it was to become a music promoter. He played guitar and flirted with the rock scene, but music was never a serious career option despite keen media interest in his association with the Ugly Rumours rock band.

It was during his first year at St John's College that Blair developed a fledgling interest in politics that would give purpose to his nascent Christianity. He met Geoff Gallop, an Australian on a Rhodes scholarship, who was known throughout the college for his revolutionary Marxism. By his own admission he was something of a rabble-rouser, a member of St John's 'Left Caucus' group of extreme left-wing students whose beliefs were dominated by Marxist thinking. Despite their friendship, Blair resisted Gallop's left-wing leanings:

> I went through all the bit about reading Trotsky and attempting a Marxist analysis. But it never went very deep and there was the self-evident wrongness of what was happening in Eastern Europe.[2]

4

Nevertheless their conversations sparked Blair and when Gallop introduced him to Peter Thomson, a 36-year-old priest of the Australian Anglican Church (reading theology at St John's) there was the first fluttering of a politico-religious awakening.

> I had always believed in God but I had become slightly detached from it. I couldn't make sense of it. Peter made it relevant, practical rather than theological. Religion became less of a personal relationship with God. I began to see it more in a social context.[3]

Blair's late-night deliberations with Thomson and friends have become the stuff of legend, likewise the work of an absent guest whose writings were regularly scrutinized by the group. Thomson introduced them to the work of John Macmurray, a communist who became a Christian socialist philosopher who was fashionable in certain circles in the 1930s. Thomson's admiration for Macmurray's work was unqualified: Macmurray believed that faith, although about the love of God, was also about improving the human condition. (Nor was it a singular view but had echoes of the working ethos of Jesuits who continued to challenge authoritarian regimes in Latin America.) Thomson's gusto was unrestrained:

> Macmurray taught me how to think through the whole notion of religion in relationship to action. Here, we had been from the time of our theological days, involved in reflective thinking and contemplating our navels and all

5

that type of thing, trying to get yourself right with God and of course there is an important part of all that. But what became real for me was every time I was involved in action, everything came alive. The smile started to come. You saw people as they were and it became exciting.[4]

Thomson delivered a powerful message. Blair was on his way, from Gallop to Thomson to John Macmurray whose writings were to galvanize his thinking. It was the practical relevance of Macmurray that fired Blair, the idea of placing Christianity at the heart of community life that would influence his domestic and foreign policy decisions during his years at Number 10. So what made Macmurray special? What did it all amount to? And if we need to understand Macmurray before we can understand Peter Thomson before we can understand Blair, who was the man who had such an abiding influence on the former Prime Minister?

Macmurray was a postmodern thinker whose experience in the First World War formulated his thoughts about the nature of religion and its reality. He believed that the First and Second World Wars were the result of a deep sickness in the western world; ironically eliminating war was the underlying purpose of his work. By the end of the First World War he became deeply disenchanted with all institutions and refused to join any religious organization (although later in life he became a Quaker) because he, and many of his comrades, had lost faith in a society they had been fighting to preserve.

Macmurray's philosophy was based on the relationship of

the individual to society which he described as 'the philosophy of the personal'. He peddled the theory that individualism starved people of a feeling of community, that salvation lay in personal relationships, 'the idea of a relationship which has no purpose beyond itself; in which we associate because it is natural to human beings to share their experience, to understand one another, to find joy and satisfaction in living together; in expressing and revealing themselves to one another'.[5]

Macmurray refused to identify his religion with any of the churches, insisting that Christianity was about being human (a position Blair might have considered when making the final decision to convert to Catholicism). Macmurray's view was that religion was fundamental to human life but that the essence of true religion lay in creating a cohesion within communities. He never budged from his belief in friendship as the true nature and goal of personal existence, believing that societies were not defined by individuals but the other way round and, importantly, it was a principle that could be applied and fulfilled within a world community.

How close was Blair to Macmurray's teachings? The Scottish philosopher had explored prominent European thinking of the 1930s and 1940s and was persuaded that action, not thinking, was the domain of human reason. Macmurray believed that action came conceptually before thinking that was later endorsed by the deeds: it was religion's only worthwhile manifestation, he said, demanding international acceptance.

We of the West who have grown so far and so powerful, often at the expense of the rest of mankind, have now to learn that freedom is not our private possession. One thing we need, which is very difficult to achieve: the ability to see ourselves as only part of a social system which is universal: and in our freedom as the trustees of a possession which belongs of right to all men. We can preserve our freedom only by sharing it.[6]

Yet how to share freedoms with people whose lives are blighted by dictatorship and oppression without resorting to some semblance of humane intervention, military or otherwise? It was a question Blair would frequently ask himself as Prime Minister (while continuing to cling to Macmurray's communitarianism as the essence of his political credo).

Whether it was Macmurray's philosophy or Thomson's charismatic teaching or a combination of the two that galvanized him, Blair began to explore in earnest the relationship between Christianity and politics, focusing on the concept of community as the main plank of his centre-left politics.

JB: *These were pretty fundamental questions that he and his pals were debating at the time. If you think about it, the true value of the Labour Party was all about solidarity with others and lifting society to another level which was closely tied to Christian values. Tony hadn't really thought deeply about religion or politics until he met Peter and of course in the 1970s religion and politics were about as unfashionable as short-back-and-sides. He always knew that he wanted to do something with his life, become more involved with* *people if you like, but had no idea where or what or how to go about it. Then once he realized that religion wasn't just about getting down on your knees and praying, but about action, about community, he saw the sense in it, although he certainly wasn't orthodox in either his politics or religion. In the context of religion, he would always ask what was the best way to do things, not because of his Christian beliefs but because of a strict set of values that apply to all religions, Muslim and Jews as well as Christians. On the political front, he believed socialism dragged people down to a certain level, it wasn't aspirational, didn't attempt to lift people. Take the kids in the Sedgefield constituency. At best, in the early 1980s, some might become pit deputies or teachers, and that was thought to be brilliant. But the idea of going to university didn't enter their heads. University was for rich people. It was beginning to change slightly in the 1990s but Tony wanted to push the boundaries further. Interestingly though, in the process he managed to upset both the hierarchy of the Labour Party and the Church on more than one occasion. Yes, he was unconventional in many respects and totally persuaded by the notion of the community politics of his Oxford days, although – we can laugh about it now – he had no idea at the time what it meant at the coalface.*

Burton, who was knee deep in the everyday application of community, related to Blair's thinking, but observers on both sides of the political divide scorned communitarianism, denouncing the concept as woolly thinking. Sarah Hale, in her book *Blair's Community*, took the criticism further, alleging that Blair's version was delusory, that his thinking was poles apart from Macmurray.

Blair and New Labour are not and never have been communitarian, despite frequent references and appeals to
community, despite consorting with known communitarians, and despite the adoption of language and even whole
discourses used by communitarians.[7]

Hale wrote that Blair's understanding of community was not
only markedly different from Macmurray but frequently in
stark opposition to it, and only an extremely superficial
reading of his work could have led commentators, and Blair
himself, to believe otherwise. Hale's main concern was his
interpretation of 'rights and responsibilities', Blair took the
view that people within communities should have rights but
must take responsibility for their actions. State benefits, for
example, should no longer be absolute rights but negotiable
and withdrawn if the recipients refused to meet their responsibilities; the unemployed must take whatever job or training
was offered or risk losing benefit; for parents to receive child
benefit, they must meet their responsibility by sending their
children to school. The notion of 'rights and responsibilities'
seemed reasonable, but Hale points out that this was funda-
mentally contractual and contrasted sharply with Macmurray
who opposed restricting the welfare state on any grounds.
Taking responsibility for oneself was a privilege 'even perhaps
in an ideal world, a right, but certainly not a burden'. With
total optimism in the human condition, Macmurray argued
that responsibility was a precondition of freedom and, if given
the opportunity, people would grasp it with both hands.

Hale's criticism bears academic scrutiny, but in the dog-eat-dog world of politics, Blair's modified interpretation of Macmurray, together with Peter Thomson's Christian, centre-left liberal policies, were customized to accommodate the demands of the political system. In both domestic and foreign policy, Blair held firmly to *his* communitarian ideas that had been fostered by Thomson/Macmurray and fuelled by other proponents of the centre-left who were beginning to espouse the 'third way'. Critically, Blair would need to be convinced that 'third way' was politically acceptable and could help win elections.

'If you really want to understand what I'm all about, you have to take a look at a guy called John Macmurray', said Blair after he became Labour leader. 'He was influential – very influential, not in the detail but in the general concept.'[8]

The final comment in this much-quoted statement is often omitted. It was 'the general concept' that prevailed, but whether communitarian thinking helped or hindered Blair's premiership is open to question. Some say that it was an ideological excuse for an accommodation with capitalism, others that it was the rationale for his controversial humane interventionism that demanded troop deployment in areas of conflict. Others shrugged and dismissed it as being simply ineffective. Anthony Seldon wrote in *Blair Unbound*, 'His own policy preferences remained incomplete and naïve, consisting of a mish-mash of Christianity, social democracy and the vogue-ish and ultimately insubstantial "third way".'[9]

Seldon was suspicious – as was secular Britain – of religiosity and politics sitting at the same table. To express any level of Christian faith in British political life was highly suspect, and while Blair had no intention of coming out as the political agent of a religious revival, his community thinking, with its strong moral purpose, prevailed. Polly Toynbee warned that mixing God and politics was a perilous business: 'The great agnostic/atheist British majority has a queasy distaste for politicians airing religious sentiments: it only fuels their cynicism.'[10]

Whatever doubts may be cast on Blair's interpretation and effectiveness of communitarianism, the upshot was to re-kindle his interest in Christianity as a relevant force in the world. At the end of his second year he was confirmed in the Church of England by the assistant chaplain, Graham Dow (later the Bishop of Carlisle). According to biographer John Rentoul, Blair did not disagree with Dow's language of a commitment to a personal Christ but was much more interested in a practical change in society. Yet the seeds were sown. From an ivory tower in Oxford, with its precious and privileged view of the world, Tony Blair discovered an intellectual and spiritual alliance that he found satisfying even in its embryonic form. In a Fabian Society pamphlet, he reflected on the need for a theological/political alliance:

> There was a tendency at one time to think that people could live in a spiritual and moral vacuum, that you could simply stop teaching those types of values and people would make their own way towards their accommodation

with society. There were elements of Utopia in that. I think we have a more hard-headed understanding now, that these values have to be taught and learnt. You can see, as a father bringing up your own children, it is a constant problem. They don't just get to it by themselves.[11]

Nor did Blair 'get to it by himself'. When he finally left Oxford, he was like a toddler who had mastered the alphabet but had yet to string together the letters to form coherent words. Within months he was to meet Cherie Booth, the next link in the Christian socialist chain who would help mould the letters and words into a meaningful language. In Cherie he found also a lifelong partner whose interest in religion and politics matched his own and who would deepen his faith and help him make sense of the heady, philosophical mélange of his student days.

The story of the blossoming Blair–Booth romance is well documented. They met when they were both pupils at Derry Irvine's chambers. Cherie was described as one of the brightest young legal brains in the country. She was brought up in a working-class area of Liverpool in a modest terraced house with her mother and paternal grandparents; her father, the actor Tony Booth, left home when she was nine. It was a tough, insecure childhood but she was bright, determined to do well at school and a devout Roman Catholic. She joined the Labour Party when she was 16, partly for social reasons but also because of her growing awareness of the social problems that were an integral part of Merseyside life in the 1960s.

Her background contrasted sharply with Blair's middle-class, public school upbringing. When Blair theorized about the importance of community, about rights and responsibilities and Christianity best expressed through action, Cherie could claim first-hand knowledge of 'faith in action'. Her mother Gale, a fiercely independent woman, had been forced to work in fish-and-chip shops to support her family. While the family hardly suffered serious deprivation, Cherie witnessed her mother's daily struggle, bringing up a family as a single parent, the omnipresent financial insecurity, and the embarrassment of an errant father (although she was influenced appreciably by Tony Booth's socialism as well as her grandmother Vera's Roman Catholic faith). Cherie's politics and religion were etched on the same hymn sheet and would deepen in the coming years.

JB: *I used to wonder whether it was Cherie's intellect and religious beliefs that attracted Tony to her. It might have been to some extent, but it wasn't the only attraction. Sounds corny, but they were a couple very much in love and still are. When you see them together you realize what a strong, healthy marriage they have . . . more so than most middle-aged couples. And despite the problems of living in a goldfish bowl, they've brought up four lovely, normal kids who are a real credit to them.*

But beyond the love and the family and the marriage, it was also a meeting of minds. If you think of the coincidence of Tony meeting someone like Cherie after his experiences at Oxford, someone with the same mix of Christianity and socialism, one inter-dependent on the other, you have to believe it was a marriage made in heaven, or Labour Party Headquarters, whichever came first!

What's interesting though is that Tony was able to expand and develop his ideas about politics and religion, which were still in their infancy, with someone who had experienced many of the theoretical situations that had been up for discussion at St John's College. She knew about 'community politics' first hand, she knew about hardship and financial insecurity, and she knew, for example, what the Militants had done to Labour in Liverpool, and it wasn't for her. She was never extreme – probably slightly further left of centre than Tony – but she was focused, as he was, on what you would call practical, living politics, never politics based on dogma. Of course what's really interesting is that it was only after they were married in 1980 that Tony took the Labour Party seriously. They both joined the Hackney South Labour Party that same year – not the best of times in the Party's history.

1980 was a time of deep divisions. Michael Foot was elected leader of the Party in a bid to stop Tony Benn's bid for the top job: Foot was believed to be marginally more acceptable than Benn. The press were relentless in lambasting the brilliant but guileless new leader who seemed not only to have had a fashion by-pass, but suffered from a peculiar political neurosis: continuing to press for unilateral nuclear disarmament, higher taxation and the closed shop, policies that were hardly beloved by the British electorate. Two years into his leadership, Foot became acquainted with an aspiring young barrister who, in a lengthy letter to the Leader, set out his thoughts on the shortcomings of the Thatcher government:

The Tory Party is now increasingly given over to the worst of petty bourgeois sentiment – the thought that there is something clever in cynicism: realistic in selfishness; and the granting of legitimacy to the barbaric idea of the survival of the fittest.

Precociously, Blair then suggests how Foot should address the 1982 Labour Party Conference:

I would appeal for a sense of purpose in the Party. We have a duty much higher than the duty to any grouping or tendency or section of opinion within the Party. It is a duty we owe to the people in our country, to save them from a cruel and bigoted government, that has made disaster and despair a fact of their everyday lives. Over the past two years we have set an example to the country of how an opposition should not behave; we must now set an example of how it should behave.[12]

With an election just months away, the race was on for Blair and Booth to find parliamentary seats, and they agreed that whoever found a safe seat would pursue a career at Westminster while the other would become the family breadwinner. Cherie's patch was Thanet North, a safe Tory seat that Labour had no chance of winning. Months later Blair found Sedgefield. Cherie Booth's parliamentary dream was over; for Blair it was just the beginning of an incredible journey.

CHAPTER 2

Sedgefield to Westminster

One hears the language of a young man eager to please who doesn't yet know what he thinks.[1]

Critics accused Blair of being chaff in the wind: a more generous view is that he was an enthusiastic, ideological hobo, hugging the centre ground and sprinkling 'third way' ideas around like holy water. In the County Durham constituency of Sedgefield, he was to meet a man who would help transform his political fancies into living politics. John Burton, a Christian socialist and Labour councillor, was a practitioner of community politics which, in the heart of the Durham coalfield, was a way of life, a channel for improving the lives of people that local councillors represented. Blair could hear echoes of Peter Thomson as Burton preached the message: socialism is about improving the quality of community life, and religion is about helping our neighbours.

Gazing out of the kitchen window of 'Myrobella', the Blairs' constituency home, Burton observed a landscape that had changed dramatically over the years: once a heap of coal and rock, now green fields spread out and children played and, as the view had changed, he knew, too, that the Party must change if it was ever again to be a party of government.

JB: *The early 1980s was a grim time in the Durham coalfield. In Trimdon we were working on small, focused projects just trying to make tiny improvements, to help people who were having to come to terms with the closure of traditional industries: pits, steelworks, shipyards were disappearing fast. The people wanted jobs, economic stability and decent schools for their children rather than lectures on Marxist philosophy from left-wing activists, but there was only so much we could do at local level, and to be honest there seemed little chance of Labour ever winning a General Election. The Party was crippled by Militants and trade union intransigence, dogma-ridden, unelectable, and we knew it had to be taken by the scruff of the neck and shaken until the Party saw sense. The old ways were dead. We didn't need to wear cloth caps or carry union cards or, worse still, carry large chips on our shoulders. So-called militancy was a relic of old Labour. We had to look to the future as a party that would represent working- and middle-class people with aspirations that had to be met, social justice, a fair deal for ordinary people, better schools, hospitals, higher education for their kids if that's what they wanted. The only way was to strip away everything, apart from basic party values, and rebuild in a way that wasn't only achievable but could start winning elections.*

No clock had been better regulated; Burton's dream of a new brand of politics matched that of the young Blair who

believed that the constituency was an exemplar for the
Labour Party nationally:

> John and his friends already understood that our party
> must modernize to reflect better the needs and ambitions
> of the people who depended on us to improve their lives.
> John Burton is living proof that New Labour had its roots
> solidly in the traditional Labour area of the North East. It's
> why many of the reforms which helped our party win back
> the trust of the country were piloted here in Sedgefield
> under his guidance.[2]

This was May 1983. Tony Blair was on the political starting
blocks with political ambition and theories aplenty but in
need of politicizing, not only in the workings of the Labour
Party but in the aspirational might of the working class. Old
Labour, too, was stuck in a time warp, blaming the Tories for
everything and getting away with it.

*   *   *

It was a knock on the door of Number 9 Front Street,
Trimdon Village, on the evening of 11 May 1983 that kick-
started Blair's political career. If destiny is a matter of choice
and not chance, then it was a wise choice for the young
barrister who planned to ditch a career at the Bar for the
House of Commons, if he could find a safe seat. Sedgefield
was a new constituency sitting between the Rivers Wear and
Tees and carved out during recent boundary changes. The

new local party, far from being up to speed, was caught napping when Margaret Thatcher announced a snap election set for 9 June. Time was running out for local party members to find the right person to represent them.

Inside Number 9, Burton was settling down with friends to watch the European Cup Winners final between Aberdeen and Real Madrid. Together with Paul Trippet of Sedgefield Council, Terry Ward, a local councillor, Simon Hoban, Trimdon Youth Officer and Peter Brookes, a social worker, they were planning to write a leaflet thanking supporters who had helped them during the local elections. Good intentions, along with the leaflet, were put to one side as the whistle blew for the start of the match. With beer, wine and sandwiches on the table, they looked forward to the prospect of a goal-fest – a vain hope in the event – when the fateful knock on the door interrupted the match.

With a queue of prospective candidates beating a path to his door – Sedgefield was the last constituency in the country to adopt a candidate – Burton could have been forgiven for being less than enthusiastic at the intrusion. But Blair was invited in and offered a drink while the lads returned to the football action. It was an agonizing wait for the Oxford graduate and City lawyer with his well-rehearsed pitch to win their support put on hold for 90 minutes, on hold again as the game went to extra time, and again as the two teams decided the match on penalties. Two and a half hours later – and a win for Aberdeen – the television was finally switched off. Trimdon's Famous Five, as they became known, looked inquisitively for the first time at their visitor and saw a young man with a broad smile, well turned out in his best grey suit, and a hybrid, posh accent. After a brief critique of the football, the conversation switched to politics.

JB: *I still don't know why I let him come. He rang me the day before just as I was going out to work. There was something about his voice. It's hard to say. But the last thing we needed was another young hopeful on the doorstep even though we were running out of time to find a candidate. Not only was Sedgefield the last constituency in the country to adopt a candidate, Trimdon branch was last in the constituency to put a name forward. We were the last bar saloon for any aspiring candidate. The election was only a few weeks away and we had to get on with it. My name was being considered by the branch but I was happy to stand aside if the right person could be found.*

So we started putting Tony through his paces. Where did he stand on Europe, defence, the state of the Labour Party? It was an interesting session because normally, if you're going for a job you tell people what they want to hear. He didn't do that. For example, the Party was anti-Europe in the early 1980s. He wasn't. He believed we had to be in there, trying to influence policy. Then the issue that cost Labour the previous election – unilateral nuclear disarmament. It was disastrous for the Party but great for the Tory press, helping them to beef up Labour's 'loony left' image. Tony admitted he had flirted with CND but decided disarmament was a no-hoper. Neither view was popular at the time. And he talked about his ideas for change, the need to broaden the Party's base, which is exactly what we were doing in Trimdon. His ideas were like balm in a party hell-bent on self-destruction. And he also

21

happened to be very good on his feet. He had this impressive ability to think through an issue and, with his lawyer's training, analyse it, taking it to the bitter end. We liked what we were hearing. But it was more than that. It was his manner that won us over. He had a presence about him that I knew instinctively could win elections. There was a kindred spirit. He didn't talk about his religious beliefs, other than mentioning the Christian socialist group that he'd been part of at Oxford and how much the experience meant to him, and we didn't push him on the subject because it didn't seem right, but we felt we could trust him. We all did. Even Paul Trippet. At the time Paul was working on a building site, an ex-member of Militant, an unlikely Blairite you might think. Yet he was sufficiently convinced to take two weeks off work to show him the area. Tony had that charisma if you like.

Before agreeing to support Blair, there was one important matter to resolve. Trippet took Burton aside and said that, while he was impressed with Blair, he thought Burton should go for it himself.

JB: *I said no, I can't win it, a prophet is never recognized in his own land. In truth, I was ambitious. I could have done the job but would never have achieved what Tony's achieved. So I've no regrets because, to an extent, I've fulfilled my political ambitions through a close association with the Prime Minister. As it was, it was easier for me to get Tony selected than putting my own name forward. To the people of Sedgefield I was John Burton, councillor – a good councillor, but a councillor nevertheless.*

Once Burton decided against throwing his hat in the ring, Trimdon's Famous Five agreed to support Blair for the Sedgefield seat. And if faith moves mountains, there was a hefty mass to shift. They had nine days to get Blair's name on the shortlist. Beyond the first hurdle there was a major battle ahead to win the backing of the Executive Committee of the Sedgefield Labour Party, at the time dominated by left-wing activists. In theory, Blair had no chance of winning the nomination. Did Neil Kinnock and Roy Hattersley approach two of the most powerful trade union leaders in the North East to secure the seat for Blair? Was it strong-arm union tactics that won the day? Burton accepts that the unions were useful but denies that the nomination was a trade union fix.

JB: *Of course the unions played their part. Joe Mills, of the Transport and General Workers' Union, was very supportive. Tom Burlison, too, of the GMB. Yes, there was definitely a move by the union's top brass to stop the left winning the seat, but at the end of the day five men from Trimdon saw Tony Blair, liked what we saw and set out to sell him to the constituency party. If the unions played a part, it was about agreeing not to put up centre-left candidates of their own. Remember, on paper this young man hadn't the remotest chance of getting the nomination because at the time the local Labour Party was dominated by left-wing people who had their own candidates lined up for the job. What helped, though, was that people were slowly beginning to think about what was happening to the Party and asking questions about why it was doing so badly and looking for an alternative. It was our job to show we had found a damned good alternative.*

23

The campaign was tough. Blair moved in with John and Lily Burton and the house became an embattled campaign head-quarters. As Lily recalls, the young parliamentary candidate soon became one of the family.

> We only had three bedrooms so the children used to take turns sleeping on the floor. When I look back I wonder how we managed, but it was all a big adventure, with lists and notices and issues and to-do lists pinned to the walls. Yes, it seemed chaotic, but in fact we were highly organized. We had to be, and it turned out well in the end, despite the agonizing wait to see if we would get the nomination. I remember the night Tony's name was added to the shortlist and the next day the candidates were going to be grilled by the Executive Committee. John went off that night to our local church to pray, and the next morning Tony took himself to Durham Cathedral, neither telling the other . . . that's just the way it was.[3]

Once Blair had been selected, there was little time for quiet meditation, and despite the chaos and the obvious drawback of a short campaign for a new candidate, Blair won with a respectable majority of 8,281 votes, a personal triumph which was celebrated royally at the Red Lion in Trimdon until the small hours of the morning. But there was little cause to celebrate nationally. The 1983 election was a disaster for the Party. Labour's share of the national vote fell to 27.6 per cent, just ahead of the Liberal/SDP Alliance on 25.4 per cent which was then perfectly positioned to challenge Labour as the main opposition party. For Blair, however, the future stretched out before him in the comfort zone of a safe Labour seat in his beloved County Durham, a place that would give him roots and bring him closer to traditional Labour supporters.

And if Burton gave Blair a roof over his head, it was Sedgefield's Roman Catholic priest, Father John Caden, who provided spiritual cover. Blair had been discouraged from attending the Catholic Church in Trimdon when the local priest delivered a strongly worded, anti-Labour sermon. Angry at what he regarded as a personal attack, he refused to set foot in the local church again and on Sundays insisted on making the ten-mile round trip to Sedgefield. Unusually for a Catholic priest, Father Caden was also an Independent county councillor, but, more than his politics, he was a skilled tennis player.

When I first met him, Tony was lodging with the Burtons. He told me his wife was a Catholic and asked if he could bring her to Mass. Of course I said yes. Anyway I thought he was a canny reader so I asked him to help out on some Sundays, doing some of the readings. Then we started playing tennis on Saturdays, usually doubles, and in between we used to talk about all manner of things – religion, politics; he was quite intense, very little small talk.

I remember he started out as a very chivalrous tennis player. We used to play for the exercise and have a bit of a laugh and in between games we'd put the world to rights, as friends do. But as time went on, I noticed the change in his game, noticed the steel that came into his every shot.

Whether the change in his tennis matched his promotion through the ranks of the Party, I never did work out. But Tony liked to win. Oh yes. He liked that.[4]

In Sedgefield, Blair had the complete package, a safe Labour seat, a political mentor and a tennis partner-cum-spiritual adviser. But it was time to head south to Westminster to meet the new member for Dumfermline East, Gordon Brown, who over the years would become a close friend and a sullen rival. In the early months Blair and Brown shared a pokey office in the Palace of Westminster, and despite being markedly different characters were destined to become the indomitable Labour Party modernizers who would discard old Labour dogma, steal the Tory mantle from under its nose and dominate Britain's political landscape for more than a decade. (Subsequently some believed that bringing the two men together was more than a coincidence, that it was the work of an astute observer in the Whips Office who saw them as the Party's future hope.) Yet the modernizing duo had some distance to go before the electorate would trust them sufficiently to hand them the greatest electoral triumph for a century. But, to quote Father Caden, 'Tony liked to win. Oh yes. He liked that.'

CHAPTER 3

MP to Leader of the Labour Party

The Labour Party is like a stagecoach. If you rattle along at speed everybody inside is too exhilarated or too seasick to cause any trouble. But if you stop, everybody gets out and argues about where to go next.[1]

Labour's three election defeats – 1983, 1987 and 1992 – hardened Blair's view that only grass-roots reform would bring electoral success. Labour's 1983 manifesto had been riddled with contradictory policies that had lurched further to the left under Michael Foot's leadership, a cauldron of incompatibilities that included withdrawal from the European Union, wholesale nationalization of major industries and banks, unilateral disposal of Britain's nuclear deterrent, a party in denial that turned a deaf ear to the wishes and aspirations of the electorate. Change within the Party was vital if it was to win power and reduce the growing gap between rich and poor. However, the Conservatives believed they had little to fear from the opposition, could dismiss it with the flick of a little finger, a government lolling on its political laurels with a healthy 144 majority.

Yet it was the best of times for Labour newcomers. Labour was in such a dire state that the tiniest contribution to its recovery was noticed and welcomed. Blair made the most of the opportunity, steadily soaking up ideas, his singular climb up the parliamentary ladder all the more remarkable given his outsider political status and lack of allegiance to any party faction.

The political rock, to which he returned faithfully every weekend during his early parliamentary career, was his constituency. What he saw happening in Sedgefield endorsed his view that Labour would never win power without a root-and-branch shake-up. Nevertheless, Blair had not fully addressed the question of *how* change would come about, other than having a strong conviction that good must prevail over evil, a belief in the importance of community and the guiding principle that people, as well as demanding rights, should accept responsibility for their actions.

A ready smile hid his concern that the Party was tearing itself apart, unfit to govern, debilitated by dogma dating back a century with its adherence to nationalization, high spending/low taxation, the closed shop, all flying in the face of the aspirations of traditional Labour supporters. Not only did the Party face oblivion but it refused to acknowledge its plight, digging an even deeper hole for itself. (Tony Benn lost his Bristol seat and welcomed defeat as a moral victory.) The dying ethos was painful to witness. In October 1983, six months after the election, Neil Kinnock replaced Michael Foot as leader, the first positive sign that survival might be possible. Kinnock's first act was to tear up the 1983 manifesto and start again, but if the Tories were to be vanquished, Kinnock and his team had a major battle on their hands. The dilemma was to transform the image of the Party, ditching old Labour policies that had proved so damaging while retaining some sense of unity within the Party.

While Militants continued to alienate the country and Kinnock pledged to meet the extremists head-on, Blair looked on with increasing admiration at his own constituency party reaching out to people in a stagnant political climate, priding itself in finding new ways of moving the Party forward. For example, one of Sedgefield's most controversial moves was to reject a Labour Party ruling that prospective members should be members of a trade union. Burton and his colleagues believed the ruling was unfair, that mass membership was important to the future of the Party, and they agreed to ignore the ruling despite protests from the Party. Moreover, they allowed people who were unable to afford the £15–£18 membership fee to join regardless of their ability to pay. As long as they made a contribution, no matter how small, they were accepted. It became Sedgefield's Christian crusade, a 'big tent' approach before the term 'big tent' had any political currency. Burton led several discussions in the early 1980s, often with Blair present, when he argued that if people were allowed to be members of the Party they might, in time, decide to join a union. This proved to be the case. The local branch of the Transport and General Workers' Union (TGWU) saw their numbers double, although this did little to placate the left wing of the Party. Former Cabinet Minister Stephen Byers recalls: 'Whenever we took decisions in the early days, we would all look at one another and ask the question: "Will this one be anti-Burton or anti-Prescott?" They were at opposite ends. We knew we couldn't please both.'[2]

JB: *It made sense, giving people what they wanted. Why should prospective members have to take out union membership if they didn't need membership? It was common sense, but to put it right we had to break the rules – I think we still do – and Tony was with us every step of the way. Okay, mass membership wasn't the most serious issue of the day, but insisting on union membership added to the voice of the loony left that made it difficult for the Party to be taken seriously.*

I suppose this is what Neil Kinnock meant when he told Tony that he should 'Sedgefieldize' the Party after he became leader. We were New Labour before the name was invented. Looking back over the past 25 years I can't pretend to be neutral. I was part of the process that created New Labour. We'd taken a lot of stick from the left who just wouldn't accept that if they continued down that militant road, we would be dumped in a big black political hole. Why did it take so long for the Party to learn lessons? The British will always shy away from electing an extreme party. Yet Militants believed that they were the principled ones and we were selling our souls to the devil. But what good would it do if the so-called principled ones never gained power? It wasn't principled. It was stubborn arrogance. The centre ground was the only place to be and we proved it with three glorious election wins. I always said to Tony, 'Press on with what you're doing. Don't be side-tracked. Don't move towards the Party. Let the Party move towards you.'

In those first months though, the Commons took some getting used to. Of course Tony had some way to go before his political thinking matured, but he was constantly seeking advice and talking to people of all political persuasions. In a way it was a distinct advantage not being tied to traditional party dogma because he would have never achieved as much as he did if he was constantly dragged down by 'It-must-be-this-or-that-because-it's-always-been-that-way' brand of politics. There were no emotional hang-ups, not like Neil who wore his heart on his sleeve. But they had a good working relationship despite their differences, and there's no doubt he saw Tony as front bench material early on. But Tony thought differently from Neil, thought about issues on the basis of need, not because they were party dogma.

Some still say it was a definite weakness – the fact that Tony wasn't immersed in traditional Labour thinking. Yet when we interviewed him for the job, we saw it as a strength because we were certain that the Party needed a new direction. We were desperate to move on. Tony believed, as we did, that to make the Party electable we had to broaden our appeal and steal the centre ground because by this time, people were sick to death of the Thatcher government and nervous of old Labour and the left. But he still needed to refine his thinking, flesh it out, if he had any chance of convincing others.

Just weeks after his thirtieth birthday, Blair became Labour's youngest MP. His maiden speech was not the best of his parliamentary career, vague and rather gauche as he outlined his brand of socialism:

It stands for co-operation, not confrontation, for fellowship not fear. It stands for equality, not because it wants

31

people to be the same but because only through equality in our economic circumstances can our individuality develop properly.[3]

It was a promising if dull start for Blair. He raised questions on unemployment, not only the indignities of being jobless but demanding to know how the unemployed could afford to get married, start a family and access benefits that ought to be taken for granted. In 1983, when the harsh language of Militants was common usage, any mention of marriage and starting families in a political context was rare. The Macmurray echo was audible:

What the unemployed need is not pity from a distance but their bare rights as members of an astonishingly wealthy community. We have to see that they get their rights and not pat ourselves on the back for our benevolence when we are merely being honest and decent.[4]

For the next decade, Blair worked hard to make his mark both inside and outside the House. Outside the Chamber, he targeted influential members of the Party, members of the press and business leaders, keeping an ear to the ground for political whisperings. He continued to speak about politics in moralistic terms. With his crisp 'Vicar of St Albion' voice, he would denounce moral relativism, reminding the world that Christianity was a tough religion. There was right and wrong, good and bad, and although he avoided sharing his personal religious beliefs, invariably they emerged as covert ethic-speak, repeating the message that values were what mattered and implementing them was essential. Membership of the Labour Party for him, he liked to remind people, was a matter of choice, not traditional family thinking. He had joined the Party because he shared its fundamental values, 'Co-operation not confrontation, fellowship in place of fear.'

Despite his political statelessness, Blair was to rise rapidly through party ranks. Within a year he was promoted to Labour's front bench Treasury team, moving on to City and Consumer Affairs, Energy, and Trade and Industry spokesman before the 1987 General Election. With Peter Mandelson in post as Director of Communications, the founding team of New Labour was in place, although each had different priorities.

Whereas Brown and Mandelson, both single men at the time, would spend evenings mulling over policy in their cramped Westminster office, Blair would escape to his young family; Euan was born in 1984, Nicholas arrived the following year and Kathryn was born in 1988. Three pregnancies in four years, plus a successful law practice, meant that Cherie was forced to abandon her political ambitions. Nevertheless, she remained fully supportive of her husband's career and continued to be an active member of the Labour Party, elected to the Executive of the Labour Co-ordinating Committee in 1983.

JB: *A good deal has been written about Cherie's influence on Tony, that she put iron into his soul, pushing him further down the path that Peter Thomson had taken him. Certainly she encouraged him, always stiffened his resolve when it was necessary, and yes, she had very strong political views and at times they would really argue about policy. He would listen, not always convinced; but the way I saw it, she helped clarify and beef up his politics rather than being responsible for them, as some writers have suggested.*

Those early years were tough for both of them. Tony was making his way at Westminster, Cherie was getting to grips with her work at the Bar, and together they were making the 500-mile round trip to Sedgefield at weekends. They were still living with us and I often think back to that time when I see Cherie being pilloried by the press. She's been an easy target. I remember her as a young, married woman, very much in love with her husband – and she still is. I remember we only had two single beds to offer them, but they didn't care. They used to put a couple of mattresses together and sleep on the floor. We would pretend not to notice.

A few years later, when the family was growing up, they would all go to church together on a Sunday. Tony liked the idea of it being an occasion for the family and had no hang-ups about going to a Catholic church. When the press were speculating about him converting after leaving office, he would say, 'Why should I? I'm happy as I am.' But I often wondered how he felt when Cherie and the children would take Communion together and he was left behind in the pew. I don't think he liked that very much.

As the family got older, Blair became more and more uneasy about his outsider status in church, although Father Caden said the question of taking Communion was never an issue.

I can honestly say that I never saw his attendance at Mass as a first step to conversion. It never entered my head. He was still very much in thrall with Peter Thomson and continued to attribute his Christianity to Peter, never his parents. I suppose I took it for granted that he was an Anglo-Catholic who had promised to bring up his children as Catholics. And he never received Communion at my church or expected to.[5]

In a magazine article on the fusion of faith and politics, Blair set out his view that Christian churches were 'hardly free of blemishes' and should never claim or pretend moral superiority. Despite the blemishes: 'Christianity means we are not stranded in helpless isolation but owe a duty both to others and to ourselves. The act of Communion is symbolic of this message. It acknowledges that we do not grow up in total independence but interdependently.'[6]

So for Blair the act of receiving Communion was more than being a family at prayer. It symbolized community, interdependence and never feeling excluded. However, his impatience with a Catholic ruling on non-Catholics taking the sacrament would result in a public rebuke from the highest Roman Catholic voice in the land. But that takes us ahead of our story.

*　　*　　*

By 1987, Blair, still in his mid-thirties, was seen as one of the rising stars of the Labour Party, one of Kinnock's young Turks, in the vanguard of Labour's plans for renewal that would one day endear the Party to the electorate. But for all Labour's campaigning efforts to persuade the country that the Party had changed, it was insufficient to win over new support. Despite mounting a professional campaign, Margaret Thatcher was returned to Number 10 with a reduced but respectable 102 majority. It was a telling moment for, despite Peter Mandelson's public relations efforts, the Party was left confused, confounded and rejected. Labour diehards had clutched old-fashioned dogmas to their left-wing chests and the voters responded with a resounding 'No.' Kinnock's attempts to modernize had fallen short of expectations.

'There are some of us who will fight, fight, fight and fight again to save the Party we love', Hugh Gaitskell told the Labour Party Conference in 1960. In 1987, the fight intensified. There would be no more tinkering. At the top of Kinnock's long to-do list was re-examining the Party's relationship with the trade union movement which, he believed, had seriously damaged Labour's chances of winning elections since the 'winter of discontent' in 1979.

With this in mind, Kinnock appointed Blair Shadow Employment Secretary in 1989, giving him a perfect springboard for making his mark on the Party and the country. Blair realized that it was a mighty challenge and an opportunity not to be missed. He was ready to take on the might of the left, including its deep-seated support of the closed shop whereby trade unions insisted that all employees in companies and industry should be members of a union.

JB: *We'd dealt with union membership of the Party in Trimdon but this was something else again. If he succeeded, it would be the biggest indicator yet that the Labour Party was changing and would also change for ever the relationship between the unions and the Party that had been so damaging. Of course, if he didn't succeed, it would have destroyed his reputation for ever, so there was a lot at stake. I know he worked closely with Peter Mandelson who encouraged him to go for it. Then of course he picked off the union leaders one by one to get them on side. At first they were furious, but because of the introduction of the European Social Charter, they began to see there was no easy way round it. They had to decide between the Charter that had key benefits for working people, or the closed shop. There was a backlash of course and complaints to the NEC, but eventually, after endless late-night sessions, the unions agreed to back it. I was just beginning to realize what sort of guy we'd taken on in Sedgefield, with his doggedness and determination and ability to persuade. He seemed never to flinch. I've always put it down to his strong religious beliefs that somehow seemed to stoke his self-confidence, for better or worse.*

The minutes of the meeting of the Labour Parliamentary Committee recorded Roy Hattersley's view that Tony Blair had carried off an almost brilliant coup. Anthony Seldon wrote: 'Reflecting years later, Hattersley felt that "this was the second thing after the selection (at Sedgefield) which demonstrated his steel".'[7]

The closed shop became history and Kinnock understood that he must move the Party still further away from its unsustainable position. Links with the trade union movement were loosened, Militants were expelled, unilateral nuclear disarmament was abandoned along with the 'red flag', and the red rose became the Party's new emblem. The polls looked hopeful, and days before the 1992 campaign opened, Labour was shown to have a seven-point lead. Where and how did it go so badly wrong? On election day, the British people again refused to take the final step, unconvinced by Labour's pledge that it had turned the corner of high taxation and high spend. The Conservatives, under John Major's leadership, won with a working majority of 21.

It was a severe blow to the Party's morale and to the ambitions of the MP for Sedgefield. He told the press the following morning: 'The true reason for our defeat is not complex. It is simple. It has been the same since 1979. Labour has not been trusted to fulfil the aspirations of the majority of people in a modern world.'[8]

Kinnock was forced to resign. His successor John Smith was in sharp contrast to the loquacious Welshman. Smith was a traditionalist with little enthusiasm for party reform who believed 'just one more heave' would secure victory for Labour. He acknowledged that the Party had to change, but his tortoise-style pace frustrated senior colleagues, including Blair. It was a faltering, limbo time for Labour. The Party wrung its hands and asked what more it could do to convince the country that a metamorphosis was under way. Having ditched one controversial Labour policy after another, and expelled Militants, why was the Party still unelectable? Moreover, in its feverish bid to restyle itself, had the Party become bankrupt of ideas? Was an '-ism' needed to cover its ideological nakedness? What would replace the Party's core beliefs that had been the soul of Labour for a century?

Smith appointed Blair Shadow Home Secretary. While privately criticizing Smith's lack of dynamic leadership, Blair bonded with the new leader, comfortable with their shared Christian beliefs. Smith had no qualms about publicly declaring his faith and he introduced a firm moral tone into his speeches that Blair admired (but which further unnerved Smith's left-wing colleagues). 'Politics ought to be a moral activity', Smith said in the R. H. Tawney Memorial Lecture in 1993.

In nine years as an MP, Blair had spoken endlessly about moral values in political life but had said little about his own religious beliefs. Encouraged by Smith's utterances on the importance of his faith, Blair joined the Christian Socialist Movement in 1992, a move that passed largely unnoticed. But it was an emboldened Blair at the Party Conference:

> We are trying to establish in the public mind the coincidence between the values of democratic socialism and those of Christianity. There's a desire in the Labour Party to rediscover its ethical values, the ethical code that most of us really believe gave birth to the Labour Party.[9]

Fusing Christian and socialist values had been at the heart of Labour's message in the early twentieth century, when Christian socialism began to flourish on the streets of Manchester and the Potteries, with idealists like Tawney reaching out to the poor, offering comfort and practical help. So was there anything new in linking the values of democratic socialism and Christianity? Had the British not embraced some form of Christianity since the days of King Ethelbert of Kent and through the centuries to the present Queen? But times were a-changing. Since the 1960s, Britain had become increasingly secular and the social revolution heralded a new libertarianism that rejected common moral values for individual choice.

Blair believed that the social revolution had gone too far but was reassured by political prophets who were sensing a sea change. Political movements periodically wax and wane to further or hinder the fate of major parties and the spirit of the age: Hegel's '*geist*' would once again be on the move, they said, going full circle away from the liberal swinging sixties. Yet for now, secularism was winning the battle in Europe as the established churches lurched from crisis to crisis. Any sign of the major Christian religions attempting to influence government caused raised eyebrows. Look at America, they cried, at its clawing religiosity that was, and still is, a controversial feature of the American political system. In *The God Delusion*, Richard Dawkins describes Christian fundamentalism as the American Taliban following a slavish adherence to a misunderstood old text: hatred of women, modernity, rival religions, science and pleasure; love of punishment, bullying, narrow-minded, bossy interference in every aspect of life. 'They represent what I have called the dark side of religious absolutism, and they are often called extremists. But my point is that even mild and moderate religion helps to provide the climate of faith in which extremism naturally flourishes.'[10]

Politicians acknowledged that there were large numbers of people in agreement with Dawkins and his 'dark side of Christianity', one of the main reasons why British Members of Parliament are reluctant to publicly share their religious beliefs. But the press had identified Blair as the messiah figure, labelling him the Party's new moralist, and none more so than in the wake of the horrific murder of two-year-old James Bulger in February 1993. The toddler was led out of a shopping mall in Bootle by two young boys who brutally battered James to death. Blair, now Shadow Home Secretary, was shocked to the core, describing it 'like hammer blows struck against the sleeping conscience of the country'. His speech caught the mood of a traumatized nation in what was to be one of the most emotional speeches of his career to date:

A solution to this disintegration doesn't simply lie in legislation. It must come from the rediscovery of a sense of direction as a country and most of all from being unafraid to start talking once again about the values and principles we believe in and what they mean for us, not just as individuals but as a community. We cannot exist in a moral vacuum. If we do not learn and then teach the value of what is right and what is wrong, then the result is simply moral chaos which engulfs us all . . . The importance of the notion of community is that it defines the relationship not only between us as individuals but between people and the society in which they live, one that is based on responsibilities as well as rights, on obligations as well as entitlements. Self-respect is in part derived from respect for others.[11]

41

The speech marked out Blair as a future leader as he addressed the complex question of 'values and principles' that were traditionally regarded as exclusive Tory territory. Moreover, the speech reflected the national mood of anger and revulsion, articulating issues of social concern in a way that people could relate to. Added to his recent tough stance with the trade unions, Blair had found his voice, and it was a voice of high moral tone. Labour had never been trusted on law and order, and now he was issuing an ultimatum: the Party would protect and foster people's rights, but they must also accept their responsibility to society. It was a creed that needed further refining and needed political support.

In January 1993, Blair and Brown visited Washington, a fact-finding trip to learn from Bill Clinton's historic presidential election victory. Clinton, too, had put personal responsibility at the centre of an active communitarian programme that demanded responsibility in exchange for opportunity. Clinton's team advised the two Labour MPs that the principle of personal responsibility could be applied across the board – to welfare reform, unemployment and crime. It was music to the ears of the Shadow Home Secretary. His mantra, 'Tough on crime, tough on the causes of crime', now had a philosophical base from which to operate. John Rentoul, in his biography, called it a breakthrough for Blair.

It was not until his Washington trip that anything resembling a 'great movement' became evident. Blair at last gained a sense of cohesion and acquired a language in which to express his latent 'social moralism and set of beliefs that would provide him with a distinctive platform for the leadership of the Labour Party'.[12]

Blair and Brown quizzed Clinton's team on their election win and were advised to adopt a 'triangulation' strategy, straddling left and right and going for economic growth that would be critical in pursuing a sustainable welfare programme. For Blair it provided the perfect mix of sound political positioning and vote-winning policies. Words like 'community', 'rights' and 'responsibilities' had peppered his language since the mid-1970s at those late-night sessions with Peter Thomson. And so the crusade for change was launched. Back home, Blair shouted it from the rooftops, or at least from the pages of the *Sun*, preaching the idea that a serious decline in a sense of community was the underlying cause of increased crime rates. 'It's a bargain', he told the *Sun*. 'We give opportunity but demand responsibility. There is no excuse for crime. None.'

By the start of 1994, Blair was clearly identified as the leader of Labour's modernizers while Smith faced growing criticism from senior Labour politicians who were frustrated by his eagerness to please both wings of the Party, a strategy the polls showed was leading nowhere. The consensus seemed to be that while Smith had integrity, was personable and had shown great courage, particularly over the 'One man, one vote' issue, he was not moving fast enough to secure the centre ground. His 'One more heave' approach was never going to achieve an election victory. Kinnock, however, refused to join in the groundswell that might have threatened Smith's leadership, if events had not taken a fatal turn. At a dinner on 11 May 1994, Kinnock advised John Smith that he must take control and get his message out to voters in a series of policy lectures around the country, setting out a clear strategy for the future direction of the Party if Labour had any chance of winning an election. Smith agreed and said he would start planning a series of policy lectures after the Labour Party Conference. It was a pledge he was unable to keep. The following morning, John Smith suffered a massive heart attack and was pronounced dead at 9.15am.

Blair was in Aberdeen where he was due to make a speech as part of the European election campaign. He delivered his speech, cut short his visit and returned to London amid intense speculation that he was Labour's new leader in waiting. A weekend poll on 28 May gave Blair 47 per cent, John Prescott 15 per cent and Gordon Brown 11 per cent. It was obvious, even to Brown, that a humiliating defeat would be the only consequence of a leadership bid. Brown decided, therefore, to engage in a bargaining session with Blair to see what role he would be given if he agreed to withdraw from the contest, resulting in an agreement whereby Brown would be appointed Shadow Chancellor with responsibility for economic and social policy. The two men arranged to have dinner at the Granita restaurant in Islington to work out the detail, the Blair–Brown horse trading that became the stuff of legend. In the event it would cause Blair aggravation and Brown resentment for years to come. The so-called deal cast a shadow over the entire Blair premiership, used by Brown and his supporters to show how Blair had reneged on his succession promise. Yet the most credible explanation of 'a deal' is that Blair suggested that he would not want the job indefinitely and, in time, Brown might become leader. They were words of comfort rather than a pact.

JB: *Tony always respected Gordon's ability and his background. He was the true 'son of the manse' again, a Christian socialist with a strong sense of right and wrong and a deep love and respect for his father. He was taught about community responsibilities and believed that strong communities were essential for individual prosperity. So they had a lot in common, and Tony believed they could be a powerful team. Yet it seemed Gordon couldn't forget that he lost out to Tony for the leader's job and it rankled. It was like a cancer. He became impossible to work with.*

The story of the Granita pact was rubbish. How could any future prime minister give a guarantee on when he would stand down? How could he pass on the job to Gordon? It wasn't in his gift. The truth is that Gordon and Tony met secretly at Durham County Hall where they first discussed the leadership issue. It was all cloak-and-dagger stuff, sneaking in through the back door to avoid the press. Then they had a further meeting at Cherie's sister's house to finalize it. Granita was just a dinner for two colleagues who knew they would be working closely together. But Granita was damaging, used time and again by Brownites to prove that Tony had reneged . . . supposedly a timetable for the handover and all . . . ridiculous.

With Brown's support, the only thing in question was the size of Blair's majority. The leadership election, on 21 July 1994, gave Blair 57 per cent of the vote against John Prescott with 24 per cent, and Margaret Beckett 19 per cent. At the age of 41, Blair was the youngest Labour post-war leader. For Burton who, two years earlier had urged Blair to stand, it was a high point:

JB: *It was an unbelievable feeling. This young man, who we knew had the potential to help us in Sedgefield, had become leader of the Party. Unbelievable. The tears were just rolling down my cheeks. I knew he had the ability to unite the Party and, more importantly, to win elections. He had the personality and the policies that would appeal not only to traditional Labour voters but to those in safe Tory areas. Even changing the name to New Labour might sound trivial now, but it sent a message to the country that old Labour was finished and a new era in British politics was about to begin.*

Many of those old Labour policies that had made us no-hopers had been dealt with – the closed shop, 'One man, one vote', getting rid of unilateral nuclear disarmament, ditching Militants – and had all gone some way to make voters look at Labour afresh. But research showed that there was still little trust in us as a party of government. I remember his speech to Conference in his first year as leader when he talked about the need to build trust with people, not only those disillusioned with the Labour Party but those disillusioned with politics generally. It was a clever move – pushing the mistrust away from Labour's door and implying that it was a general malaise in the country, which it was after years of Tory rule. We adopted the 'big tent' approach, meaning nothing should be allowed to keep out supporters, especially those new to Labour, exactly the approach we had adopted in Sedgefield ten years previously.

'Myrobella' also became a 'big tent'. It came alive. There was so much going on, especially as the children got a little older. The Blairs would come as a family when they could and the local kids would come round, playing football in the garden or Alastair playing cricket and a bit of fast bowling. Kids still remember it. Then there was a stream of advisers, journalists and political colleagues. But there was so much to do. Despite the diversions of cricket and football, we had to focus on one thing – making the Party electable and winning the next election, convincing voters that Labour was the reformed party they could trust.

Re-branding the Party was easy. The biggest task facing New Labour was to prove to the country that it was no longer the party of higher taxes, that it wanted to re-engage with business, that the economy would be safe in its hands, that it was no longer in the clutches of the trade unions. But was there anything left to inherit after abandoning so many traditional Labour policies? And there was the vital question of re-discovering the Party's soul, finding an '-ism', a philosophy that the Party could unite around. The new leader of the Labour Party believed he had the answer.

CHAPTER 4

Leader of the Labour Party to Prime Minister

I didn't come into politics to change the Labour Party. I came into politics to change the country.[1]

Politics and religion should never be discussed in polite company – a wise old adage because, at best, any serious analysis results in deadlock and, at worst, ends in conflict. There is also a predictable chain reaction: examining questions of faith leads to questions about truth which, in turn, leads to questions about how faith and truth can help make the world a better place. If we add politics to the mix, is it not likely that faith and truth might fall victim to a fickle political system? Now personalize the hypothesis. The saintly person will see the world as a place in which to do good in order to do penance (with the promise of a reward in heaven), while the politician with even modest Christian leanings will want to see a better world now, without awaiting the glories of the next. Such benign ambition justifies the pursuit of power and the politician's pledge to bring peace and justice to the world.

But how to fuse the two unmentionables, politics and religion, into a creed that is morally and politically acceptable?

Welcome to the 'Jesus Manifesto', the process of building a policy platform upon which a 'better world' is crafted – re-distribution of wealth, equality of opportunity, public sector reform. Politicians called it 'third way', a haven for centre-left parties, an ideological framework that steered a middle course (and seemed to have the added benefit of avoiding the electoral wilderness of the extreme left and right).

In 1994, the new leader of the Labour Party, Tony Blair, together with his modernizing team, identified 'third way' thinking as Labour's new Holy Grail. As Prime Minister, he was to flesh out his thinking in a pamphlet published by the Fabian Society:

> The 'third way' stands for a modernized social democracy, passionate in its commitment to social justice and the goals of the centre-left, but flexible, innovative and forward looking in the means to achieve them. It is founded on the values which have guided progressive politics for more than a century – democracy, liberty, justice, mutual obligation and internationalism. But it is a *third way* because it moves decisively beyond an Old Left preoccupied by state control, high taxation and producer interests; and a New Right treating public investment and often the very notions of 'society' and collective endeav-our as evils to be undone.[2]

In the months that followed, the words 'triangulation' and 'third way' became common parlance, and hard, leftist dogma was outlawed like last year's clouds. The team sought advice from a myriad different sources, ideas and policies that would lead to a modern welfare state. The strategy for New Labour's Jesus Manifesto included tackling social exclusion, mutual responsibility (a hand-up, not a hand-out), public–private partnership on welfare delivery, a re-emphasis on active welfare, not just benefits.

The list was impressive enough. No one could argue about good intent. But linking good intent with the ups and downs and the immediacy of the political system was something else again. Elections needed winning. Manifestos needed writing. Voters needed persuading that New Labour was fit to govern. And the art of the possible needed a semblance of a political ideology to make 'third way' a credible bedfellow. Furthermore, if Blair was to experience a whiff of power and demonstrate that the Party had changed irrevocably, fundamental change to the Party needed to happen quickly to persuade the electorate that Labour could deliver economic efficiency alongside improved public services and social justice.

Sprucing up the image of the Party was critical. Nothing would be allowed to obscure the message that New Labour was what it said it was – a new, soft-edged, centre-left party with radical new thinking on tax, trade union power and social welfare. But Blair was looking for something more than a superficial makeover. He wanted to make a statement, a big statement that would dazzle; ridding the Party of the esteemed but moribund Clause IV of the Party constitution fitted the bill.

The revoking of Clause IV, Labour's sacred cow, was a symbolic act to illustrate Blair's determination to tackle old Party dogma, in this case an out-of-date ruling that embodied the

Party's commitment to public ownership. It dated back to 1918 when Sidney Webb, a prominent social reformer, set down a form of words expressing the view that private ownership was exploitative and the Party would seek common ownership 'of the means of production, distribution and exchange'. Over the decades, several Labour leaders had tried to abandon Clause IV but had given up the fight: in 1959, Harold Wilson famously described such a move as 'being asked to take Genesis out of the Bible'. Blair accepted that change was not without inconvenience, but he was convinced that rewriting Clause IV would prove conclusively that the Party had reinvented itself.

JB: *If Tony had been beaten on the issue, he would have been finished, and worse, it would have been the end of the Party. It was a big, big issue for us. People started asking how Tony had become a fighter in such a short space of time, taking on the might of the unions. In a nutshell, it was all to do with his thoughts about the future of the Party and winning power. It was the right thing to do and the right time to do it. Other leaders had shied away from it, but if we had shied away from it, then we would have been facing the prospect of opposition for ever. It was a major obstacle to winning power and, let's face it, Clause IV was a millstone around our necks, a policy that would never be implemented, no matter how sentimental old-Labour activists were. It was back to that word change. Our world had changed. People demanded change, so I think the general mood in the country also helped.*

Some say it was easier for Tony to commit to abandoning Clause IV than it would have been for Neil because Tony didn't have the same emotional hang-ups about it – and that's true. He certainly didn't regard it as a tortuous process. It was just something that had to be done before the Party could move forward, and it turned out to be a defining moment for him personally and the Party. He achieved the impossible without too much bloodletting. And it was the first time that I'd seen at close quarters his relentless approach to the job. Clause IV was dragging the Party down. It was obstructive. It was wrong. It had to go. Simple as that.

Rewriting Clause IV was also an opportunity for Blair to deal with his historic victory in moralistic terms. Rather than rooting it in the socialist vocabulary of Tony Benn or Michael Foot, the new version made several references to the community and the importance of rights and responsibilities, 'the rights we enjoy, the duties we owe'. Still, the 1994 Party Conference rejected Blair's proposal by the tiniest margin, 50.9 per cent to 49.1 per cent – hardly a humiliation. Early the following year, he launched a nationwide road show aimed at changing Labour attitudes to Clause IV, and after several weeks sensed that the tide had turned. In April, a special conference voted by 65 per cent in favour of the proposal. For Blair it was a personal triumph, his 'Clause IV moment' that politicians yearn to emulate. However, the trade union movement, while reluctantly accepting Blair's proposals, remained cool, and his relationship with the TUC was never the same again. TUC leaders and left-wing politicians gave warning that ditching Clause IV – a creed at the heart of the Party for more than a century – would create a gaping void that would be impossible to fill.

After the conference, Arthur Scargill was heard to say, 'We are fighting for the very soul of the Party.' It was a battle Scargill and his supporters had little chance of winning in the urgent clamour for reform that would lead to the return of a Labour Government. Yet Scargill and other TUC leaders had, unintentionally, identified a major problem: the culling of traditional Labour policies would indeed leave a void. To many in the Party, Blair's natural inclination – to hug the centre ground – was an imperfect substitute for years of proud Labour traditions that included common ownership and trade union power.

Despite the rumblings on the left, Blair sided with those political prophets who were forecasting a period of transition. The mood of the people was on the cusp. Party activists were convinced that the next election was there for the taking in a country wearied of Thatcher's Britain, increasingly dismayed at the culture of the individual and weary of the pernicious behaviour of Militants. Like Philip Gould, Blair was taken with the idea that the twentieth century had been the 'Conservative century'. Tory governments, he reasoned, could rule from the right and be re-elected, but Labour governments could never rule from the left and secure re-election. Anthony Seldon explained:

> If he let taxes and spending rise more than the public would stand, if he pushed the European agenda too far, paid too much attention to alleviating poverty or helping minorities, or tinkered with the constitution more than was deemed necessary, then the party would suffer at the polls.[3]

If Blair and Gould were correct in their view that Britain would, from time to time, grudgingly accept progressive centre-left governments, then that time was now. Having taken on the challenge, in particular his audacious handling of Clause IV that helped push the Party ahead in the polls, Blair looked admiringly at the political transformation taking place across the Atlantic. Bill Clinton had captivated American voters with the promised reward of 'third way' solutions that had returned the first Democratic President of the United States in 12 years to the White House. Like the Labour Party in Britain, Democrats had struggled with their outmoded image. In previous elections, the Party had come up against the same brick wall as old Labour: economic efficiency was questioned, they were accused of being the party of 'tax and spend', soft on crime, and the Party that encouraged welfare dependency. The Democrats were also labelled 'the same old secularists' who shoehorned their beliefs into some form of religiosity for the duration of the election campaign (just as Labour had to contend with the right-wing view that they were largely heathen).

Clinton demolished old Republican claims, and having styled himself leader of the New Democrats, advised Blair to follow his example by broadening the appeal of Labour, adopting a 'big tent' approach and courting the media whenever possible.

JB: *Bill Clinton was a role model for Tony, there's no doubt about it. He was determined to stay close to Clinton, just as he would to George Bush. All those years at Number 10 he saw himself as a bridge between Europe and America and believed any talk of* *choosing between either Europe or the United States was damaging. There was no need to choose, and more importantly, if he was to have any influence on the international stage, then it was crucial to be alongside the President, whoever was in the White House. What was the point in standing outside? Who would listen then? His aim was to establish a special role for Britain, especially when you looked at other European leaders who were split on national issues and were militarily weak. There was certainly a great deal of respect on both sides, and from their earliest days Tony and Clinton saw themselves leading a broader movement of the centre-left because the time seemed right on both sides of the Atlantic.*

After Blair's earlier visit to Washington, there had been regular transatlantic contact between New Labour and New Democrats. A year after he became leader, Blair met the American President during Clinton's visit to London. The meeting, although low key, was a huge success. Aides say the two men found an instant rapport. There were unmistakeable similarities. Both were driven by the need to reach out beyond the traditional party faithful. Both were personable, extroverts, oozing charm when the situation demanded, and both were converts to the 'third way' message. Yes, it might be compromise politics, they would say privately, but parties won elections by taking votes from the centre ground, not by harking back to old ideologies.

Those of a more cynical disposition hinted that Blair's enthusiasm for 'third way' was bound up in his admiration for the new American president, overwhelmed by his association with 'the world's most powerful man'. Yet, once again in the telling of the Blair years, it was the coincidence of the right people, at the right time, with the right message. Whatever the cynics whispered, 'third way' was much more than Bill Clinton. Fernando Henrique Cardosa of Brazil and Wim Kok of Holland were the earliest exponents. Cardosa was well known for his work on dependency theory. Elected President of Brazil in 1994, he described himself as leader of the 'viable left'. The Dutch Prime Minister Wim Kok believed that if 'third way' governments paid attention to market needs of the new economy, they could fulfil election promises to maintain healthy welfare systems. Blair related fully to this centre-left economic strategy that allowed the market to dictate investment and jobs, while protecting and boosting health care, social security and schools.

The darling of 'third way', Anthony Giddens, insisted that centre-left parties were reacting to common issues and problems that forced a rethinking of leftist traditions. New Labour had no choice. It had to become a modernizing party: 'Modernization is not a meaningless term. It refers to the need to reshape the institutions of the country, to respond to changes that are transforming the economy, sovereignty, cultural life and the wider international system.'[4] Also striding the 'third way' platform was Amitai Etzioni, a sociology professor at George Washington University who heavily influenced American and European communitarian thinkers. Etzioni stressed that governments should avoid focusing on individual rights at the expense of individual responsibilities: a rallying call with a familiar ring, going back to Blair's Oxford days. And Etzioni was certainly the man of the moment at several courts:

Gordon Brown was said to consult him, as did the German Chancellor Helmut Kohl, President Clinton, Vice President Al Gore and Fernando Cardosa.

So what was the trigger for this powerful coalition of the centre-left that Giddens described as 're-shaping the institutions of the country'? In the area that really mattered, social reform, the consensus was that reform would take place only when long-term economic stability was secure: crucially, it was the only viable alternative to *laissez-faire* conservatism and the damaging socialist policies of the extreme left. Moreover, the new coalition came with a respected global-wide label that helped reinforce Blair's plea to move on from the damaging policies of the past by substituting a respected political alliance for the future. He put together a team to consult with Bill Clinton's advisers who persuaded them that a modernizing party of the centre-left could win, not only in the US, but also in the UK. They were heady times, and Blair's admiration knew no bounds when, in 1997, Clinton won the White House for a second term. This was the moment when the seeds of Blair's ambition were sown – to win a second historic victory for New Labour – even before he had managed to win his first election.

A year into his leadership, Blair called on his old Oxford mentor Peter Thomson who had returned to Australia, and asked him to join him in London. Thomson responded generously and spent the summer of 1995 discussing Labour's proposed Manifesto with Blair and his inner circle. The tone of the discussions in those idyllic summer days can only be surmised. What we know is that the Labour leader was convinced he had a credible strategy which needed an injection of intellectual beef before it could become the basis of New Labour's election campaign. After endless hours of discussion with Thomson and others, including Peter Mandelson, Gordon Brown and an army of focus group advisers, Blair's next task was to convince the Party that 'third way' thinking was an election winner and would sweep Labour to Number 10. Thomson's contribution was persuading Blair that 'third way' could also be New Labour's missing '-ism', the Party's new ideology and the means of rediscovering its soul.

JB: *We had focus groups in Sedgefield back in the 1980s. And whenever he came back to the constituency, Tony would bounce ideas around, looking for approval, asking us to test ideas within the local party. But we had to remember that our local lad was party leader now and likely to become prime minister. We took the task very seriously and we knew what made our people tick. These were people whose political lives weren't just about sitting on committees or distributing leaflets. Let's face it . . . their politics had been formed by a pretty tough way of life. Yet if someone in the community was in need, we were there to help. Helping one another was what we did. Where I found it difficult – still do – is in separating that sort of community politics, if you like, from anything that the Church might be saying or doing. In a small community, they become one and the same thing, and no one questions the source of the action or the motivation of the do-er.*

Tony often said that some of the policies we pursued at local level were needed at national level. Labour in Sedgefield, he would say, was a big Party with roots in every part of the community.

What Tony wanted, of course, was a big Party with roots in every part of the country.

'Third way' rights and responsibility was part of our deal in Sedgefield. If you take as a tiny example – but one that was impor-tant to us – we were very proud of the sports and community centre that we'd built in the village. Everybody was made welcome, no matter how much they could afford, but if anyone stepped out of line, they'd be barred. After all, Jesus threw gamblers out of the temple. And we'd throw them out of the sports centre if they broke the rules because you have to be tough in applying them . . . it's about demanding that people are responsible for their actions. Whether there's a distinct Christian strand in there I'm not sure, but it becomes interesting if you take it further. Apply the same principle to the man who refuses to pay his taxes or neglects his children. Religion has always been associated with order and fairness and retribution. So questioning traditional Labour views on benefits, for example, and demanding responsible behaviour from the recipient sits comfortably with Christian thinking. As Christians, though, we should never forget to provide a safety net for those people who for a number of reasons will never be able to take responsibility for them-selves or their families. As Tony said time and again, Christianity is a tough religion. It's not a cosy option. It's about right and wrong. But the principle of the whole community working together makes sense, achieving what individuals can't do on their own; and it also made sense on a national scale. Of course the Tory way is just to shrug your shoulders and walk away.

1994–7 was not, however, about breast-beating or publicly proclaimed beliefs; it was about winning a General Election.

After four Labour Party defeats, Blair was haunted by the notion that the country would fall back on its traditional right-of-centre voting pattern. His faith may have comforted him when black thoughts came to him at dead of night, but what he desperately needed was the support of the press, of the business community as well as the Party faithful. Every opinion poll was scrutinized for the slightest movement up or down, with senior Party members shamelessly on the side of Mammon, trying to convince voters that Labour could be trusted with the economy. It was a tough call – to overturn the Tory claim that the economy could only be safe in the hands of a low-tax, low-inflation party.

Courting the press was crucial, and in September 1994 Blair appointed Alastair Campbell as Press Secretary. Campbell was political editor of the *Daily Mirror* and a keen supporter of Blair since they met in the 1980s, who wanted to be part of the New Jerusalem (despite his avowed atheism). Campbell knew all about the vagaries of the press pack, how the pack worked and how damaging certain stories could be. From day one at Number 10, no opportunity would be allowed to slip by in the battle to change media perceptions of New Labour. Not only was he media spokesman, he became minder to the relatively inexperienced leader, instilling caution into his every word and move.

Among Campbell's many quotable quotes – most were peppered with expletives – the most pithy was to David Margolick of *Vanity Fair* who, when pressing Blair on whether his foreign policy decisions had been shaped by his religious beliefs, was told quite firmly, 'We don't do God.' Campbell had never been more serious; he opposed any public profession of Blair's faith (biblical quotations in speeches were given the red pencil). On a flight to Germany, where Blair was due to speak at Tübingen University, Campbell writes in his diaries: 'On the plane, we worked on the speech and I was trying to get the religion out and more politics in.' In Blair's damaging speech to the Women's Institute, Campbell pleaded with him to make drastic changes to the script. Blair said he wanted to balance old and new, put the responsibility agenda up alongside opportunity as the twin pillars of community. Campbell was unequivocal: 'It was drivel, including a paragraph, which at one point TB included, about the new being a glittering sword and the old a sturdy shield.'[5]

In 1996 Matthew d'Ancona of the *Sunday Telegraph* persuaded Blair to talk about his Christianity. In an astonishingly personal interview, he described himself as an 'ecumenical Christian' and agreed that religion had shaped his political thinking. He said he found it difficult to understand the argument between Protestant and Catholic that he described as a battle from the past. His strong sense of right and wrong was explored as he discussed sin and the tragedy of alienation from God. Again he drew on his understanding of John Macmurray, the Christian stress on community and the emphasis not on a relationship with God but relationships with one another. 'This is the essential reason why I am on the left rather than the right', he said.[6]

Campbell was furious. It was naïve to think that, no matter how sincere Blair had been in discussing his convictions, they would be well received by the press. Campbell believed that his boss was courting disaster. The next day's headlines were highly damaging: according to Blair, only those of the left could be good Christian folk. Conservatives were essentially doomed. 'Party political point scoring', 'Sanctimonious', 'Philosophically weak', 'Mere religious opinionating' were just some of the verdicts (although no one explained why secularism was synonymous with reason while religion was mere opinion) but Campbell felt vindicated:

> I said to TB, 1. Never believe journalists when they say they are doing you a favour or giving you a free hit. 2. Never do an interview without someone else in the room, and 3. Never talk about God. Hilary (Coffman) and David (Hill) felt it wouldn't play too badly, but I sensed a mini-disaster as it was Easter and they were trying to spin this as Blair allying Labour to God. When you looked at the words, he didn't say that, but he said enough to let them do the story and get Tories piling in saying he was using his faith for politics and saying you couldn't be a Tory and a Christian. This was the permanent risk with UK politicians talking about God.[7]

Blair accepted he was wrong and vowed never again to discuss religion. He was virtually gagged on any direct questions about his faith although succeeded in weaving Christian messages into speeches that could be linked to community and shared values. In a high-profile speech at Tübingen University, with the Catholic theologian Hans Küng by his side, Blair threaded his way through the politics and faith debate:

If it is true that it can only be clear commitment to shared values that we survive and prosper in the world of change, then surely religious faith has its own part to play in deepening such commitment. What is faith but belief in something bigger than self? What is the idea of community but the national acknowledgement of our interdependence? In truth, faith is reason's ally.

Religion has often resulted in bigotry. But so has political ideology. However, a society where there is religious faith will always, in my view, be inherently more likely to pursue the good of humankind; and the less it sees reason as its enemy, the quicker it will get there.[8]

Blair appeared to modify his Christian Socialist thinking, finally suggesting to the Tübingen audience: 'The modern welfare state is not founded on a paternalistic government giving out more benefits but on an enabling government that through work and education helps people to help themselves.'

Was this the same ethical socialism that Blair had always espoused? Was it a 'third way' compromise that Christian Socialists could accommodate? And how did it match up to Macmurray's opposition to governments restricting the welfare state in any circumstance?

'Third way' thinking sat comfortably with Macmurray's communitarianism at a philosophical level, but the differences became apparent in the delivery of state benefits. Rights would no longer be seen as absolute rights because benefits would come with a price tag. The welfare state was also creating a section of society that had become disincentivized, an underclass dependent on benefits. What about the unemployed who received benefits without condition and whose families were adequately housed, fed and clothed? What incentive did they have to better their lifestyle or that of their families? Why grapple with the world of work when the state was there to provide? Was there an inkling, a modicum of socialism in New Labour's argument?

The left, privately outraged at the departure from traditional Labour Party thinking, dared only whisper its opposition, although there were one or two diehards who openly snapped at the ankles of the reformers whenever the opportunity arose. 'We may win elections from time to time, but all that is worthless unless our thoughts and actions are firmly grounded in moral truth', Tony Benn retorted.[9]

Blair welcomed the debate. It was important to acknowledge, and even boast, of the differences between old and New Labour because Labour's past spelt failure. Yet preaching ideas of 'third way' and 'triangulation' and 'renewal and reform' demanded that they have shape and substance. One answer to what otherwise might be seen as a hollow offering, was Labour's welfare-to-work programme that dominated the agenda in 1996 and became the New Deal programme. Instead of cash, New Deal offered places on employment schemes, training and education; in return the unemployed were required to take up the opportunities or risk losing some of their benefits – 'a service that offers people a hand-up, not just cash payments, rather than giving them a hand-out'. The traditional Christian Socialist belief that it was the state's duty to unconditionally provide welfare benefits was no longer in play; the intention was to see the underclass rising into an aspirational working class (reflected in the Conservative policy of selling council houses). A contributing factor was Philip Gould's focus groups, who were reporting to their political masters that higher taxation would not be tolerated. People were not prepared to increase their contributions to the needy.

The reality of top-flight politics was kicking in. The shift from centre-left to the middle ground was under way (and some distance from Macmurray's non-contractual thinking). Interestingly, the French Prime Minister Jospin was one of the few European leaders to cling to the rhetoric of a socialist past: 'We are not liberals of the left. We are socialists.' It was a brave attempt, but Jospin failed to attract middle-class voters who had flocked to Clinton in the United States and were about to flock to Blair's Britain because Blair never forgot that there was an election to win.

Was there anything new in Blair's repositioning? In his book, *Arguments for Socialism*, published in the 1980s, Tony Benn wrote that the teachings of Jesus were not necessarily weakened by being secularized – a view supported by Keir Hardie, the first leader of the Parliamentary Labour Party who described socialism as 'the embodiment of Christianity in our industrial system'. Yet to those on the Christian left, there remained a spirit that transcended both the secular and the industrial system, a moral responsibility rooted in religion that provided the ultimate rationale for socialism with no room for compromise. But with the prospect of an imminent election, few dared express their disquiet publicly.

Blair was beginning to realize that, like Pontius Pilate, 'he had to be both principled and expedient'. The interview with Matthew d'Ancona provided an intriguing insight into Blair's mindset when he spoke of his awareness of Pilate's dilemma, torn between belief and political reality: 'One can imagine him agonizing, seeing that Jesus had done nothing wrong, and wishing to release him. Just as easily, however, one can envisage Pilate's advisers telling him of the risks, warning him not to inflame Jewish opinion.'[10] Blair called it a parable of political life, the responsibility of the decision-maker that came under intense scrutiny during his premiership, when he addressed moral issues, family, abortion, cloning. Over a period of ten years, on almost every count, Blair backed the secular liberal view rather than that of robust Christian teaching. On abortion, Blair never once voted with the pro-life lobby and voted 14 times with the pro-choice lobby in Parliament. In December 2000 he gave personal backing to regulations permitting stem-cell research on human embryos, and his government enthusiastically promoted the 'morning after' pill. The amiable 'third way' President Cardosa of Brazil believed that decision-makers were in a no-win situation:

As a politician your responsibility is to change reality and not just defend principles. If you're committed to change you cannot turn an ethical position into an obstacle for action. The problem is that, as an academic you're trained to tell the truth, but a politician is taught to lie or at least omit. As a politician, if you say everything you want, you never get everything you want.[11]

67

Blair's liberal pro-choice stance brought down the wrath of Church leaders. One of the most virulent attacks came from Cardinal Thomas Winning, the Catholic leader in Scotland who, despite being one of Margaret Thatcher's harshest critics, launched a high-profile campaign during the 1997 General Election to force Blair to prove his faith by banning abortion. However, Winning's outburst did little to damage the untouchable Blair, who simply explained it as the difference between public policy and private morality on delicate matters of conscience.

(In his 1960 presidential campaign, John F. Kennedy dealt with similar criticisms: 'I believe that in America where the separation of the church and state is absolute, no Catholic prelate would tell the President – should he be Catholic – how to act, and no Protestant minister would tell his parishioners how to vote.')

Blair discussed the dilemma with Sedgefield parish priest, Fr Caden:

Yes he would agonize about these issues, but it's a clash of conscience that goes back many centuries, the duty of a politician to legislate even though it might clash with personal belief. Certainly Tony was against abortion, but as a young MP and later as Prime Minister he didn't believe he had the right to legislate against someone else's conscience. But people are very quick to judge on these very sensitive issues, and at the end of the day only God can judge.[12]

Like Pontius Pilate, Blair easily accommodated matters of conscience and political reality; above all else, he was in the business of winning a General Election and had cast his net wide to make Labour a party of government. On 17 March 1997, John Major finally obliged and announced that the General Election would be held on Thursday 1 May.

A military-style campaign was unleashed with a stark warning to MPs to stay 'on message'. New Labour's pledges were modest, printed on something the size of a credit card and mailed to every house in the land: principally that income tax would not be increased and spending would be strictly controlled, something of a U-turn election pledge for the Labour Party. But it had the desired effect. Voters of the right and middle ground were both impressed and persuaded that Blair was 'a moral force' who would not let Britain down. The press were likewise persuaded. *The Times*, *The Sunday Times*, even the *Sun* and *Daily Mail* backed his campaign, and if criticism was heard at all, it came from the left.

Given a unique level of support from Tory press barons and the Party's runaway lead in the polls, Blair nevertheless worried that the Party might find it impossible to remain united throughout the six-week campaign. Would the Party fall apart at the last hurdle? Would the electors accept New Labour's promises that trade unions were under control, that the economy would be safe in their hands, and that tax levels would remain unchanged? Had he brought about a magical transformation that five years earlier seemed impossible?

In his pre-election briefings, Blair pressed home the extent of Party reform:

The purpose of New Labour is to give Britain a different political choice: the choice between a failed Conservative Government, exhausted and divided in everything other than its desire to cling on to power, and a new revitalized Labour Party that has been resolute in transforming itself into a party of the future. We have rewritten our constitution, the new Clause IV, to put a commitment to enterprise alongside the commitment to justice. We have changed the way we make policy and put our relationship with the trade unions on a modern footing where they accept they can get fairness but no favours from a Labour government. Our MPs are now all selected by ordinary party members, not small committees or pressure groups. The membership itself has doubled to 400,000, with half having joined since the last election.[13]

It was an impressive do-good list, and voters warmed to it.

JB: *Election day was a blur. It was a strange campaign anyway because we had to run the campaign virtually without our local MP who was all over the country. I was there in Sedgefield, but of course the people and the press wanted Tony, not me. On election day itself, 'Myrobella' became the meeting place for family, journalists and advisers, but the atmosphere was weird because we all knew we were way ahead in the polls, but daren't say so. Tony insisted that we shouldn't be over-confident. To the last minute he kept saying that we mustn't presume anything, we mustn't be complacent. There were so many imponderables like turnout, lack of confidence, a last-minute middle-England panic, anything – the* *sky might fall in! In the evening, I remember driving to Newton Aycliffe and meeting Tony and the rest of the family on the steps of the leisure centre. Inside, as the results started coming in, it became obvious that predictions of a landslide were correct. Tony sat in the corner looking quite stunned. He kept saying, 'This can't be real.' At one point he even said: 'I hope the others win some seats.' On the television they were predicting a majority of over 150 and he kept saying 'This is crazy.' He was in shock at how well Labour was doing even though the polls had been in our favour for weeks. Perhaps he was a bit superstitious. If he started believing the polls, they were bound to be wrong. Eventually I asked, tongue in cheek, if we could start celebrating yet? Surely as the seats started tumbling to us, we couldn't still be accused of complacency? He managed a little smile, just the hint of one. Later, in the Trimdon Labour Club, when I introduced him as 'the next Prime Minister, our own Tony Blair', the crowd went wild. It was a proud moment . . . a wonderful, wonderful feeling.*

On the small plane down to London to claim his crown, there was a strange sense of the quixotic. The results were still coming in. Safe Tory seats were tumbling to Labour, and Blair was heard whispering to Cherie, 'But I've never been in Government. What have we done?' When the counting was over, Blair had a majority of 179, the biggest election landslide since 1931. Publicly he declared his commitment to the country and gave thanks to people from both ends of the political spectrum. Privately he was overwhelmed at the prospect of what lay ahead.

Walking into Number 10 was daunting. While Cherie and

the children examined their new home, Blair and his inner circle got down to the business of government. There was much to do if New Labour was to hit the ground running. The Party had won a landslide victory by appealing to voters' aspirations, and now it was time to start addressing those aspirations (although focus groups reminded the new government that people wanted realistic pledges rather than extravagant promises that would lead only to disappointment).

As the cheers from the crowd dimmed and people started ambling home from the Downing Street 'love-in' on Labour's first day in office for 17 years, Tony Blair pondered the enormity of the task ahead. The Conservatives had been roundly defeated. Labour had secured the most decisive victory for more than 60 years. Expectations were high given the scale of Labour's parliamentary majority. And the new Prime Minister, who was about to celebrate his forty-third birthday, had never run a single department in his life. It was the unknown. In the months and years ahead he would have to get by on his natural charm and communication skills, with continued support from his close-knit group of advisers, as well as relying heavily on his Christian faith without which, he was to say later, he could never have survived ten years at the top.

PART 2

CHAPTER 5

Domestic Policy

He (Blair) did not, like Gladstone, wander the night streets of London looking to redeem the souls of prostitutes, but he did write with the starch of a parson invoking the awfulness of moral relativism.[1]

The new Prime Minister was in a state of shock. Blair, the youngest Prime Minister since Lord Liverpool in 1812, had never been in government, had never had access to the secret contents of a red box and, equally unknown, was the mindset of a band of sacred and powerful Whitehall civil servants. To add to his woes, the team of new senior ministers likewise had no experience of government.

Preoccupied with the business of winning the election, insufficient thought had been given to what lay beyond victory on 1 May 1997: preparing for government had taken second place to the election campaign. Moreover, Labour's landslide victory meant that traditional Party supporters sensed a whiff of revolution in the Westminster air, while others eagerly awaited the first signs of Labour's promised public service reforms. It was as Blair predicted: he was saddled with a majority that looked like being a poisoned chalice. Expectation was rampant. It was time to deliver. But what, and to whom?

The 'what, and to whom?' was the crux of a much wider issue. Blair was leader of a centre-left Labour Party that, to traditional Labour supporters, had become rudderless. Root and branch Party reforms of the 1980s and early 1990s were necessary to make the Party electable but had strayed significantly from the socialist policies of its founding fathers. Bubbling beneath the surface was the cry that the heart and soul of the Party had been gouged out. Moreover, there was little in Blair's background that traditional Labour supporters could identify with, the son of a Tory atheist who became a Christian socialist, lacking traditional Labour fervour offering liberal Christianity in its place (an important distinction when assessing his premiership). Undoubtedly Christianity was the spiritual prop that brought comfort to the new Prime Minister and the spur for implementing change that would give a strong, social purpose to his premiership. But how would it impact on policy-making? Would the country benefit from a government led by a Prime Minister who operated within the constraints of a highly developed conscience?

In those first few months, Blair was a well-meaning novice, bristling with 'third way' ideas and solutions for delivering a fairer society but unsure of the extent of his power, unsure what he wanted to do with it once he found it, and, by his own admission, unsure of the top job. In general terms, 'third way' meant rejecting right-wing demands for the government to keep a healthy distance and rejecting left-wing pleas for more central control. Abroad, 'those values of community' translated into interdependency of nations and countries working together to enforce global values. The key to Number 10 would finally unlock Blair's community and 'third way' policies: he believed that the world was in greater need than ever of Macmurray's vision.

On the steps of Number 10, on the morning of 2 May 1997, he set out the government's main objectives, 'a world class education system in which education is not the privilege of the few but the right of many, creating a competitive economy of the future and modernizing the NHS'. He said he would seek to restore trust in politics which should always be about service to the public. 'Today we are charged with the deep responsibility of government. Today, enough of talking, it is time now to do, time to live out the campaign slogan that "things can only get better".'

European leaders looked on enviously at Blair's impressive election win, claiming New Labour's victory as an endorsement of their own 'third way' politics. Wolfgang Merkel, the German political analyst, observed that 'the debate about "third way" had become the most important reform discourse in the European party landscape'. Blair's victory boosted their confidence and spirits. Social democrats in several European countries had been out of office almost as long as the Labour Party in Britain: now old-style democracy was on the way out and modernity ruled. A road map for New Democracy had been drawn up resulting in amazing electoral successes simply by rejecting extreme left and right ideologies and persuading voters to change their traditional voting habits. The idea of state provision was dwindling and new Social Democracy acknowledged the change. In the meantime, New Labour's positioning pulled the rug from under the feet of the Tories and heralded the demise of the Conservatives' claim to be the natural party of government.

The Government's first Budget on 3 July 1997 was a mélange of moderate ideas of Middle England. Gordon Brown vowed that his budgetary measures would make Britain 'fair, modern and strong'. Key themes were investment, the welfare-to-work scheme, education and skills, economic stability – a one-nation Budget showing prudent financial responsibility for the long term along with plans for social reform. An extra £1.3 billion was allocated for schools and £1.2 billion for the NHS.

JB: *I've often wondered how different Labour policies might have been if Neil had become prime minister, a great man and a caring politician whose whole life and background was the Labour Party – and an atheist. Is it right to think that Tony's religious beliefs were the spur to helping the disadvantaged in the late 1990s? Would a Kinnock government have targeted education and the NHS and the unemployed? Of course it would. It seems arrogant to suggest otherwise. No, Neil would have followed a similar course of action but for different reasons . . . from a deep-rooted socialist commitment to helping the working classes that had been with him from boyhood. With Tony, it came from religion and politics – politics that could hardly be described as socialist, and religion which I can't help but believe added another dimension to those* *early policies – the minimum wage, pumping money in to a decrepit health service and schools, tackling crime. Compassion, love, caring – yes, but total belief in what's right and what's wrong. It makes a difference because it forces politicians to consider people who are outside the box. It's not Labour, or Marxist or socialist. It's not a commandment of the National Executive or Party Conference. It's an inherent Christian belief that people should be treated fairly and given equal opportunities across the board – although Tony took a hammering for it on occasions. He applied that same principle in everything he did – from establishing the Social Exclusion Unit to ethnic cleansing in Kosovo, and ridding Iraq of the evils of Saddam Hussein's rule.*

Comparisons with Kinnock inevitably lead to the age-old question: do we need to believe in God in order to do good? While some see religion as freeing the political system from cynicism and free-market forces, others see it as polluting politics with fear and intolerance. Was Kinnock's compassion and desire to deal with social issues and inequalities any less valid, given his disregard of an Almighty? Richard Dawkins addresses the question of religion and goodness in *The God Delusion*:

I suspect that quite a lot of religious people do think religion is what motivates them to be good, especially if they belong to one of those faiths that systematically exploits personal guilt. It seems to me to require quite a low self-regard to think that, should belief in God suddenly vanish from the world, we would all become callous and selfish hedonists with no kindness, no charity, no generosity, nothing that would deserve the name of goodness.[2]

The National Secular Society that campaigns vigorously against religious influence in government goes further: 'Religion should be a matter of private conscience for the home and a place of worship. It must not have the privileged input into the political arena where history shows it to bring conflict and injustice.'[3]

Yet Blair believed that, without religion, there could be no absolute standards of morality. How could governments otherwise place markers when addressing crime, poverty, education? But his eagerness to place religion at the heart of government policies unnerved many of his parliamentary colleagues who agreed that, too often, there was little or no distinction between Blair's compassion and piety, and for any government, moral absolutism was a tough call. Blair agreed it was a hard line to pursue. In his 'scars on my back' speech in 1999 to the British Venture Capital Association, he outlined the difficulties in trying to deliver Labour's election shopping list, blocked by the clubfooted pace of Whitehall, which was mired in the belief that 'It's always been done this way, it must always be done this way': 'You try getting change in the public sector and public services – I bear the scars on my back after two years in Government. Heaven knows what it will be like if it is a bit longer.'[4] It was a cry of utter frustration at Whitehall's bureaucratic machine.

JB: *Yes, Tony found the mechanics of government frustrating. I've watched him on scores of occasions and he was always happiest working an audience or taking whatever was thrown at him during Prime Minister's Questions. Someone described him as an acrobat politician and I think that's right. He often said later that he was disappointed with his first term of office, not exactly wasted opportunities but not maximizing the potential either. I suppose it was lack of experience and getting to know the ways of the Civil Service. He used to say that he'd ask for something and they'd give a thousand reasons why it couldn't be done. But he was right when he said in a BBC interview that for the first 12 months the government operated as though it was in opposition, which was sad because Tony was very popular with the public and the press and in his constituency. He could have done almost anything he wanted, yet it wasn't as easy as it might have appeared. What he wanted to do more than anything was to prove that New Labour was fit to govern. I remember him saying on the night of the election how worried he was about the size of his majority. It would raise expectations, there would be calls for an all-out revolution. And there was never going to be a revolution. It wasn't Tony's way.*

'Tony's way' was packaged in Christian wrapping paper. A direct line was established between the Christian Socialist Movement and New Labour. Graham Dale, the Director of CSM, said at the time, 'We were convinced more than ever of the need to bring Christian Socialist voices to bear on policy, and we're excited by the receptiveness of Government to listen to us.'[5]

CSM's influence in government circles blossomed as a direct result of Blair's active Christianity (and that of John Smith) which was highly valued after the succession of Godless leaders. The CSM was suddenly in vogue, but was it a temporary fancy of the Labour Party or a must-have accessory to keep the political master happy? Blair wanted to believe that Britain was experiencing a genuine upsurge in ethical politics as an antidote to Thatcherism (epitomized in her unfortunate comment that 'there was no such thing as society') but it would take a leap of faith to believe that Labour politicians had suddenly turned to God at a time when secularism was robust and church attendances were in decline. As one Labour insider observed, the number of Labour MPs on the road to Damascus in 1997 wanting to make the world a better place was nothing short of a miracle.

Wanting to make the world a better place was never going to be sufficient. The Government was being forced to defend the legitimacy and efficacy of 'third way' thinking. One newspaper described it as a form of benevolent pragmatism, 'a policy that asks, is it good, does it work?' For this reason it was hated by the old left and the old right, the old right because they never did anything that was good and the old left because they never did anything that worked. And Polly Toynbee in the *Guardian* snarled, 'The third way is utterly redundant. It is in any case an escape from self-definition – a butterfly always on the wing', a philosophy that has no essential core because 'it temptingly offers the best of all possible worlds'.[6]

Whatever the weight of the criticism, 'third way' continued to fit perfectly Blair's centre-left politics. It made sense in a new world that cried out for a moral framework, a world in which individual expectations had risen and new fears had taken root. One of its main strengths was the value of community and 'third way' had two other vital components: it sat comfortably with his Christian conscience and it won elections.

What was it? Did it defy definition? 'From what is written about this debate in Britain, one would get no sense that it is a worldwide phenomenon or that almost all centre-left parties have restructured their doctrines in response to it' said Giddens, although the 'worldwide phenomenon' was difficult to qualify.[7] Was it like the Loch Ness Monster – frequently talked about, but did it really exist?

Doubts may be cast on the existence of the monster, although 'third way' not only existed but its influence was spreading across Europe and the Americas. National leaders were jumping on the centre-left bandwagon. Joining Clinton, Blair, Wim Kok and Cardosa were Gerhard Schröder of Germany, the Bulgarian President Petar Stoyanov and the Italian Prime Minister, Romano Prodi.

So how did it translate into political action? Certainly 'third way' thinking was difficult to communicate in the rapid response age of 24-hour news coverage and a cynical press. Yet in Blair's Britain, 'third way' became a useful political umbrella under which the Party and institutions could be changed for ever, marginalizing the political thinking of the extreme left. But the chorus of protest became ever louder: what did 'third way' actually contribute? In fact the checklist was impressive. 'Third way' established that investment in public services and sound economic management were not contradictory activities. It established that the welfare system was not simply a distribution point for passive benefits but was linked to individual responsibility. It established that public–private sector partnerships could work together to deliver public services. Education was regarded as the lever of opportunity. Tough on crime and the causes of crime was also key. The implications of globalization were debated. Finally, 'third way' dented the commonly held belief that in Britain, while the Tories were cruel and efficient, Labour was caring and incompetent (although Labour still had to prove that it could be both caring and competent). These were all strong, positive messages that sadly seemed to go astray, lost in the torrent of Blair's rhetoric about 'building a new and better Britain', 'creating an idyll for our children and grandchildren', 'extending the hand of friendship beyond national barriers', 'the butterfly always on the wing'.

Surprisingly, the Party remained united, in public at least, but the honeymoon was short-lived. As Ministers waited for the economy to come good, reality checks came in the form of tight spending constraints which meant that departments were struggling to deliver election promises. An added complication was that under the previous administration, pay in the public sector had fallen behind the private sector, which made it difficult to make headway in the short term: improving schools and hospitals depended on addressing the serious shortage of teachers, doctors and nurses. Ministers had little room to manoeuvre, reduced to making piecemeal changes to create the impression that reform was taking place. Another three years of 'sticking plaster' remedies lay ahead before the government began to address the question of adequate funding.

'Where were the strategies?', asked political correspondents. 'Twenty-four hours to save the NHS', 'Education, education, education'. These were slogans, not strategies. It was a baptism of fire for the Prime Minister who was unaccustomed to press criticism. Blair understood that much more investment was needed to make significant improvement in public services, but, ever the prudent Chancellor, Gordon Brown insisted that increased spending was in the gift of the Treasury.

JB: *This was the first of many disagreements between Tony and Gordon. It was time to give specific commitments on spending, but Gordon kept Tony at bay. More than anything, he was anxious to be seen as a cautious Chancellor and show the world that public spending would never get out of hand. But we had grossly under-estimated how much needed pouring into hospitals and schools, and it needed a huge injection of funds. It wasn't until 2000 that spending increased significantly on health and education, and it was the windfall tax on the utilities that helped us on our feet. I think Tony realized, then, that it might have been unwise to raise expectations in the short term when in reality it would take many years to see real improvements.*

It was just the start of the stand-off between the two of them, and in my view it was probably the biggest mistake of Tony's premiership not to move Gordon, possibly to the Foreign Office, when he had the power to do it. Why didn't he? At the height of his popularity he could have done anything, including moving

Gordon, but he chose not to. Then when he thought seriously about it in the second term, it was too late. Truth is, Gordon was building a separate Treasury empire, hell-bent on keeping Tony out. At Budget time he would keep his cards close to his chest; at times not even the Prime Minister knew what was to be announced. If they met in a corridor, he would walk past Tony without speaking. He had to be physically restrained on one occasion when he got into a temper over an election campaign issue. Resentment was eating away at him because Tony was Prime Minister and he thought he should have been. The frustration for Tony and other Ministers was that they were constantly being pinned back by the Treasury when so much needed doing. What a sad waste of talent because, make no mistake, Gordon was talented, formidable as Chancellor but so insecure and inadequate in many ways.

Was it Christian charity that stopped Tony from dealing with Gordon, who had been one of his closest friends and allies? It could be, but I doubt it. Christian charity didn't stop him sacking Peter Mandelson twice, and arguably, Peter and Tony were even greater friends. No, I think he genuinely believed that Gordon was doing a good job as Chancellor and, more to the point, knew there'd be a blood-bath if he tried to get rid of him. He didn't fear the man, but he didn't want to split the Party.

But it was sad to see Gordon, who was doing a good job at the Treasury, carrying out a vendetta that became so damaging over the years. Think what might have been if they had worked together, not sniping and building separate empires. Year by year the trust seeped away. And this was the son of the Manse, consumed by ambition and envy.

Philip Stephens, associate editor of the *Financial Times* and author of *The Making of a World Leader*, believes that Brown's intellectual intensity and grasp of political strategy were matched by his ruthless grip on power. He quotes one senior official who worked for him observing 'that the Chancellor was a politician cut from the same unforgiving cloth as Russia's Vladimir Putin, and those colleagues foolish enough to challenge Brown's decisions soon found themselves agreeing with that assessment'. Stephens argues that the analogy missed the complexity of the man. 'Behind the iron determination lay disappointment and insecurity.'[8]

Despite internal wrangling, Tony Blair committed the Government to a programme that was a genuine attempt to 'better serve the people'. There were child benefit increases, a minimum wage was introduced in 1999, restoration of free eye and dental tests for pensioners, and an increase in spending on health and education. The New Deal was launched, paid for from the windfall tax, and Working Families Tax Credit was introduced in 1998. However, with one eye on right-wing critics, Labour also cut the standard rate of income tax from 23 pence to 22 pence in the pound, cut support for asylum-seekers – a Budget that turned out to be a confusing mix of policies in danger of pleasing no one.

Was this a Prime Minister still unsure of himself and his use of power? Colleagues say he would wince at the level of poverty, misery and oppression, and genuinely searched for new ways of speeding up measures to reduce the gap between rich and poor (specifically the Social Exclusion Unit). But Blair, who rarely took his eye off the opinion polls, continued to be wary about alienating the right, particularly the right-wing press, and his caution, more than anything, greatly limited progress.

On the domestic front, Blair also wanted to achieve what every prime minister had attempted to achieve for the past 100 years – solving the 'Irish Question' and bringing peace to Northern Ireland. Yet the Irish question, with all its problems of tribal bitterness and sectarian violence (which will be addressed in the next chapter) was to prove more do-able than the multi-faceted task of improving public services that had been starved of investment for two decades. It was this crucial task of improving public services that Blair's political adviser and pollster, Philip Gould, returned to time and again as he monitored the ebb and flow of public support for New Labour. There were two guiding principles, said Gould: to reduce the national debt and stimulate economic growth; and second, with a strengthened economy, to plough money into education, health, crime and welfare. And Blair had a third guiding principle that related to the previous two – winning a second historic election victory on the back of economic competence and improved public services.

*   *   *

The story goes that in May 2000, while Blair was on paternity leave bonding with baby Leo, Philip Gould, the man who described his job as telling the Prime Minister what the public really thinks, interrupted the baby-bonding sessions with a few home truths. After three years as Prime Minister, people found him out of touch. 'You are not focusing on the domestic agenda and your language is wrong.'[9] Gould also warned that he was seen as lacking conviction, too concerned with spin and presentation. These were harsh words for the doting dad. Resisting the temptation to shoot the messenger, Blair listened carefully to Gould's advice because, unlike many of the yes-men and women that surround all prime ministers, he refused to tell the Prime Minister what he might prefer to hear. Hard truths were an intrinsic ingredient of Gould's vocabulary.

In what sense was he out of touch? Why did Gould feel the need to tell the Prime Minister to stop hiding behind Downing Street's well-protected doors? What had happened to Blair's natural charm and powers of persuasion, the man who thought himself 'just a regular sort of guy'?

Gould believed that the main issue was Blair's preference for foreign rather than domestic issues. Although he had been elected to improve welfare services, build new schools and put more doctors and nurses into hospitals, people perceived a Prime Minister who preferred striding the international stage. It was true. Foreign policy fascinated him and, if Gordon was happy to look after the shop, Blair could look after the world (in the first three years of his premiership, Afghanistan, Kosovo, Sierra Leone). But here was one of his closest aides admonishing him, warning him to man the home front or New Labour would suffer the consequences.

Like Bill Clinton, Blair had given a solemn undertaking: once the economy was back on course, New Labour would invest heavily in public services that would help put people back to work. Like Clinton, he continued to use the revised language of a 'third way' leader. He talked about rights and responsibilities, social inclusion, opportunities, community. But unlike Clinton, it took Blair some time to translate the language into specific domestic policies (held back by Labour's election pledge not to raise income tax). Revenues had to come from elsewhere – in the event from indirect taxation, Gordon Brown's creative budgetary skills that were labelled 'stealth taxes'. Now three years into the first term, New Labour could boast steady economic growth, low inflation and the lowest unemployment rate for 25 years. By 2000, a large budget surplus meant Labour's earlier spending promises could be met and, in the process, Blair could prove to a sceptical business world and right-wing press that Labour could be trusted with sound economic management. Was this his answer to Gould?

In part. But economic competence was only part of the solution. There was another hurdle to overcome if the Prime Minister was to make real progress on the domestic front. A complex Whitehall system, whereby individual departments seemed to act independently from the rest of government – and from one another – was always going to be an impediment to progress unless a cross-government approach could be put in place. In 1997, the Social Exclusion Unit was set up to target poverty and social exclusion and to improve the life chances of the most disadvantaged in society. The idea was to link the various government departments and demand joined-up thinking that would promote joint action between Whitehall and the Government, shifting the focus towards prevention. A number of initiatives aimed at breaking down bureaucratic barriers were introduced. Blair agreed to head up the Unit himself.

What could be more central to his faith than launching an assault on the cruel web of factors that created pockets of intense deprivation? This was communitarianism at its most powerful, a Christian doctrine that cleared the lines for people to develop their full potential and who might need government support and resources along the way. Gould's observation that he was out of touch might, therefore, have seemed unfair, but he accepted the basic message that he had taken his eye off the ball. His close advisers pressed hard to persuade him to spend more time on initiatives like the Social Exclusion Unit.

The Unit was the brainchild of Peter Mandelson, applauded by Christian leaders even though Blair rebuffed the Church of England when it lobbied for a place on the SEU board. Nevertheless, the Christian Socialist Movement saw it as a means of working in tandem with government to define specific social need and as evidence that Blair was putting religion at the centre of New Labour policies. But key civil servants and advisers were becoming increasingly uncomfortable about God's central role in the Prime Minister's political life. Unlike America, where hearts and souls are worn on presidents' sleeves, tight-lipped officials cringed at the idea of politics and religion converging, of making public something so personal, so non-British, so soft-bellied.

A political backlash to the SEU was inevitable. It took little time for the old left of the Party to attack the plan. The Unit was dismissed as yet more Blair rhetoric, another centre-left policy that lacked substance. The term 'social exclusion' drew derision from disillusioned old-style social democrat Roy Hattersley. New Labour, he said, had substituted an anodyne term for what the left had always called poverty. Yet the phrase was coined by sociologists, not New Labour, and was meant to conjure a raft of factors that prevented the disadvantaged from being part of a wider society – not just poverty, not just physical and material deprivation, but other issues linked to health, education and income distribution.

JB: *We talked about the problem of social exclusion on many occasions. A decent society needs a government that opens doors for the disadvantaged. It's the cornerstone of any community. Tony believed passionately about individual worth – whether it was Kosovo or Kensington – and wanted to find a way of dealing with people who were excluded from society, for whatever reason. He was also frustrated by the slow Whitehall process that held back his plans to tackle isolation, the British underclass, the no-hopers. The Social Exclusion Unit was Labour's answer to the black hole that suddenly appears when individual departments don't look beyond their remits, not seeing what other departments are doing, not acting together for the benefit of all. Given his busy schedule, in Kosovo and Northern Ireland and elsewhere, Tony insisted on heading it up himself. He really believed it was a way of speeding the delivery of policies that would help those most in need – although two years later he had to admit that progress was slow. But he kept going. Three years later he set up the National Strategy for Urban Renewal in an effort to take the poorest communities up* *the prosperity league. This was his way of reducing the gap between rich and poor, although sometimes good words ran ahead of good deeds. But that was the political process, not a lack of commitment.*

The SEU was part of Blair's continuing commitment to balancing left and right ideologies, despite the reluctance of the left who were openly questioning whether it was a serious political philosophy. It was fine to see Labour turning its back on the free-market ideology of the right, they would say, and on the tax-and-spend solution of the left. But what exactly had been put in its place? The whispers were becoming ever louder. Business leaders, too, began grumbling about stealth taxes, the public were demanding promised reforms, and newspaper editors had had enough of being supportive. In any event, it was more fun returning to the attack.

Blair was conscious that the first term had not produced the radical reforms promised in 1997. However, in a speech in his Sedgefield constituency on the eve of the new Millennium, Blair strongly defended Labour's two and half years in power. He said 800,000 children had been lifted out of poverty through increased child benefit, the Working Families Tax Credit, the Sure Start programme and the new Children's Fund; the aim was to abolish child poverty within a generation. The tone of his speech then changed as 'with the starch of a parson' he set out his policies and the progress of the Government in the context of his religious beliefs.

For all the cynics and the critics who, because all the country's ills have not been put right overnight, insist nothing has changed, I defy anyone to deny that on social exclusion, poverty and third-world development, there is now a different Government in Britain today, governing with a different set of values from our Conservative predecessors.

Britain might not be the mightiest nation of the twenty-first century in size or population; but it can be the best, it can be the beacon to the world. Not only in taking to the challenge of the new economy but in developing a modern civil society built around tolerance and respect where different races, creeds and religions live side by side in harmony with each other.

Nations that succeed will be tolerant, respectful of diversity, multi-racial, multi-cultural societies. Faith is important for people and will remain so. But faith is at its best when allied to reason and tolerance. Indeed, what better start could there be to the new Millennium, marking the most important event of one religious faith, than if religions, like nations, start to reach out across traditional boundaries and achieve greater understanding of each other and what they share in common values?[10]

It was the speech that slipped through Alastair Campbell's secular net: 'religions like nations reaching out across traditional boundaries', 'faith at its best when allied to tolerance and reason', 'races, creeds and religions living side by side in harmony'.

94

This was Blair unleashed, baring his soul and using the Millennium moment to tell the world, 'Faith is important for people and will remain so' – meaning faith was important to Blair and would remain so. The speech also highlighted the Government's efforts to deal with social exclusion and poverty, Blair's 'Jesus Manifesto' that had resulted in the introduction of new partnerships, Health Action Zones, Education Action Zones and the New Deal for Employment.

JB: *The idea was to bring new resources and opportunities to some of those communities that were in greatest need. Tony had seen for himself some of the dire problems in his own constituency, here in Trimdon living cheek by jowl with deprivation, unemployment, inadequate housing and schools. We talked about the importance of faith communities as a buffer against people being socially excluded because the Church is often the one remaining community-based organization in deprived areas. Being a member of the Church can motivate people to help themselves, develop new services that meet local needs. It takes the edge off their feelings of helplessness and isolation and promotes self-sufficiency. But government action also has to be in place to support these community-based initiatives, and Tony was well aware of that. Whether it got the recognition it deserved, I'm not so sure. Some saw it as Blair's 'third way' piety, but it made a difference, especially to the level of child poverty, although the question will always be asked, was it enough?*

Blair's Millennium speech fitted the Peter Thomson mould, with religion, community and political action binding together. At about the same time as Blair's speech, Thomson said in an interview on Australian television:

> I think as far as Christianity is concerned, it's all about being earthed. At the end of the day it's worth it because no matter how frail we might be, we can still do something, and if we just make a little contribution, it's more than nothing. And it's more than that kind of awful cynicism that people wallow in, and it's just not good enough. As human beings, we're more than that.[11]

It is easy to see why Thomson wielded so much power and influence over Blair. Thomson made reference to the 'social gospel', the new world crying out for a moral framework in which individual expectations had increased. Blair had taken the message on board. If people were aspirational, deal with their aspirations. If people wanted more choice, give them more choice. And to those who believed that government action was insufficient, he could hold on to Thomson's words, 'If we just make a little contribution, it's more than nothing.' But as much as Blair felt the need to deal with social exclusion issues, poverty and reform, his heart was set on achieving a second election victory. At times the dream paralysed his actions, as he cautiously sought to offend neither left nor right.

JB: *Yes, there are two sides to this – the need to win elections and the campaigning that leads to victory and power. The other side of the equation is about winning the trust of the people and involving* *them in the process of government because, at the end of the day, as Tony reminded us non-stop, if you don't have the people on side, you don't have power, and if you don't have power, you have nothing. Even Dennis Skinner, the darling of the left, would say to Tony privately that although he thought the Government hadn't gone far enough in redressing the balance between rich and poor, at least Labour had addressed some of the issues that concerned him . . . the minimum wage, social exclusion and changing the whole notion of what kind of society we want to be. For example, equality or inequality is not just about jobs and income but how people make use of the opportunities on offer. Someone who wants to leave school at 16 and find a job and has no interest in further education is in a different position from his neighbour who wants to go to university but can't because the family can't afford it. The important thing is the question of choice and having equal opportunities for leading life to the full, which is precisely how you manage to get people on side.*

By the year 2000, Labour were governing with a different set of rules and values from the Conservatives. And it was beginning to pay off. Large sums of money were allocated to the NHS and schools. The economy was sound. So, again, what was it that had filled Gould with such foreboding that he felt obliged to gate-crash Blair's bonding time with Leo? Despite an economic upsurge and unprecedented investment in public services, Gould was concerned that the Government was still deemed to be ineffective in tackling key issues. Two months later he penned a private note to this effect that was distributed to Blair, Brown, Mandelson and Campbell. The memo was a frank analysis of the Government's record in which Gould expressed the view that it was out of touch on crucial issues, on crime and asylum-seekers; more hurtful still, that the Government was perceived as failing to deliver on the National Health Service and that the New Labour brand was 'badly contaminated'. Gould concluded that if nothing changed, Blair's massive majority would be slashed, leaving the result of the next election 'too close for comfort'.

Intended for Blair's inner circle only, the memo was leaked to the press. Blair was incandescent, convinced the leak was designed to undermine his premiership and the work of an avenging Opposition still smarting from their loss of power. (Paranoia ruled. Journalist Nick Davies revealed in his book *Flat Earth News*[12] that the leak was the work of Benny the Bin Man who was paid by newspaper editors to raid dustbins and happened to come across a copy of the memo in Gould's bumper black rubbish bags.) But away from Benny's prying eyes and behind closed doors, the main concern was that the Prime Minister was spending too much time on foreign policy and had unwisely handed responsibility for public service reform to his Chancellor. To hold on to his lead in the polls, he needed to commit more time to domestic issues. Gould's wake-up call was disturbing. Blair took the advice of his trusted political strategist and pledged to devote more time to public sector reform. An election loomed. 'A lot to do. A lot still to do' was the message during the 2001 General Election campaign. The fight for the second term was under way.

Never before had Labour won two consecutive full-term elections. This was the drive that propelled Blair and his team into action. Accusations of endless spin were fair, but the harsh lesson of Neil Kinnock's bid for Number 10 – whose campaign was seriously undermined by the press in 1992 – loomed large in the minds of the Blair team who were adamant that history would not repeat itself. And the strategy paid off. The British electorate voted to give Blair a second chance, with a reduced majority but hardly significantly so: 167 compared to 179 four years previously.

In a speech on the steps of Number 10, a muted affair compared to 1997, Blair said he hoped that he had learnt from the mistakes of his first four years as Prime Minister: 'This is a mandate for reform and for investment in the future, and it is also very clearly an instruction to deliver.'[13]

There could be no more excuses, no more rhetoric, just the endless chore of invigorating Britain's ailing public services. Although levels of public borrowing and the national debt had been cut significantly, schools, hospitals and transport all cried out for New Labour to honour their election pledge to match economic efficiency with an even greater injection of funds into the welfare state. The people had returned a Labour Government but were restless for Blair to keep his side of the bargain. It was time to deliver. For his part, he promised to take on another 30,000 doctors and nurses and an extra 10,000 teachers, there would be more money for the police and the rail network. But the measures presupposed that Middle Englanders would be prepared to pay more in taxes to fund reform and that the iron fist of the Chancellor could somehow be prised open to release at least some of the contents of the public purse.

Blair accepted that he had been unwise to imply that significant improvements to public services could happen in the short term and regretted, too, he had not done more in his first term while his popularity and political standing had been so high. The real test of his premiership lay ahead and, although New Labour had succeeded in burying its dogma-ridden past, it needed to fashion a future. Political commentators agreed that the Government had been hemmed in by its lack of reforming zeal, preferring caution to action, stymied by its pledge to keep to Tory spending plans and, moreover, that Blair's reliance on 'third way' politics was insufficient in guiding and developing a credible strategy. However, Blair had invested too much time and energy in centre-left politics to retrace his steps and, with a second election victory under his belt, self-belief was at an all-time high. The voters, he said, were reassured by his clear moral pronouncements and strong leadership abroad.

Whatever criticism had been directed at the first term, 'third way' gave him a second chance and a second term to come good. He was said to be 'happy and content' for the first time but still needed to address the creeping scepticism and unease about his ability to head a reforming government. The second term would be different, ensuring delivery and offering choice and diversity in public services. In education, the emphasis would be on transforming secondary schools; in health, he promised to boost spending to the EU average; in crime, the former Director General of the BBC,

John Birt, was brought in to produce a report on the pattern of offending and on the criminal justice system's ability to counter crime. Philip Gould wrote to one Labour supporter:

> You may disparage the economic prudence of the first term but it is this that enables the government to sustain investment at record levels in the second, despite the world economic down-turn. The New Labour of the second term is not the New Labour of the first term or of opposition. It was new and is new again. Not perfect but better than most of us dared to hope.[14]

Anthony Seldon saw a 'more impressive figure' emerging after the 2001 election:

> Blair took some bold steps in his first term, above all the Good Friday Agreement in 1998, and Kosovo in 1999. But the bulk of his policy decisions did not come until after 2001 with the long drawn out evolution of his 'choice and diversity' agenda on public sector reform, on Europe, after he abandoned the Euro in favour of a liberalizing and activist policy agenda, and with his advocacy of greater urgency to combat climate change and poverty in Africa.[15]

The second term also saw renewed efforts to create a policy of participation and dialogue, although Labour's social policy continued to be based on 'common sense' rather than political ideology. On the question of equality, for example, the old Labour touchstone, Blair redefined what it should mean to the Party. It did not and could not mean that everyone should be the same, but it meant, despite the differences, everyone should be treated equally and be able to make the most of their opportunities. For Blair, this was central to Christianity, for the Gospels say that everyone is equal in the sight of God: equality of opportunity became a party mantra. Not surprisingly, it was issues such as equality of opportunity that added to his reputation for pursuing values rather than policies, a reputation that continued to dog him, despite his determination to press on with a public sector reform 'choice and diversity' agenda. But the criticism missed the point. Blair consistently refused to be tied down by *any* political dogma, as his 'Clause IV moment' had shown.

Looking back over the early years of the Blair government, it is hard to escape the conclusion that his religious beliefs, combined with his resolve 'to do the right thing', made it difficult for close colleagues to absorb and deal with his moral absolutes. Time and again he would say in interviews or speeches, 'I may be wrong, but that is what I believe.' Time and again he sought virtue as well as statesmanship. Peter Mandelson said that to understand Blair you have to see him in action in any given situation. 'He first of all thinks of what is the right thing to do and then the best way to communicate it.'

The moral choices behind his political decisions – defeating poverty, equality of opportunity and a strong community-based philosophy extending beyond national boundaries – made Blair's good intentions hard to fault: missionary zeal, however, made him appear judgemental and uncompromising. Issues and solutions were right or wrong, and self-belief often prevented him from listening to and taking the advice of colleagues.

If taking a hard line was necessary on any issue, it was Northern Ireland. Blair despaired at the hideous problem of sectarian violence in the province where religion had been the root cause of bitterness and hatred for generations. It was an affront to his faith and to the British people who were sickened at the sight of Christians tearing one another apart on their doorstep. Ending the violence and bringing the two communities together in peace and harmony was a priority. In the turmoil of the province's bitter religious war, Blair's self-confidence and composure were instrumental in moving ahead, one step at a time, towards a settlement. Hundreds of hours of tortuous negotiations would have to take place before a peace formula was found that would be acceptable to both sides (fortuitously signed just two days before Blair announced his resignation). But if a single issue defined the Blair years, it was peace in Northern Ireland, a quest that had eluded every prime minister for more than a century – Catholic and Protestant sharing power for the benefit of both sides of the political divide.

CHAPTER 6

Bringing Peace to Northern Ireland

All changed, changed utterly. A terrible beauty is born.[1]

Twentieth-century Belfast was the 'terrible beauty', a city where Protestants and Catholics threw stones, then bombs, at one another; where bigotry rather than godliness infected hearts and minds, and barbed-wire fences kept the two communities apart. Breaking down decades of entrenched sectarian hostility flew in the face of the province's stormy past. Republican and Nationalist activists operated on different planets, repeatedly warning there would be no sell-out, there would be no power sharing, there would be nothing less than a united Ireland. Three decades of undiluted madness resulted in 3,700 violent deaths in the province, an indiscriminate IRA bombing campaign on mainland Britain, and stoked hatred that surged through Irish veins like venom. 'Good fences make good neighbours', they cried. But segregation was crippling the community, a place where few people could be happy unless they hated and damned those on the other side of the divide.

Northern Ireland's spirit and economy were haemorrhaging. Secular observers wrote books and made television programmes highlighting the divisiveness of religion. Richard Dawkins observed, 'Without religion there would be no labels by which to decide whom to oppress and whom to avenge. And the real problem in Northern Ireland is that labels are inherited down many generations.'[2] In 1997, none would have believed that the province stood any chance of peace; more likely, it was several generations away from a negotiated settlement.

Prime ministers throughout the twentieth century had made forays into Northern Ireland politics, then side-stepped the tortuous issues that dogged the peace process. The new Prime Minister, who regarded the religious divide as anachronistic, vowed to move mountains to resolve the 'Irish Question'. There was also a secondary issue: pursuing peace would show the wider world Blair's determination to adopt consensual politics in the most embittered, tribal part of the United Kingdom.

The former Conservative Prime Minister John Major made Northern Ireland a top priority in the mid-1990s. Major struggled valiantly to bring about a settlement, but negotiations had limited success, mainly because of opposition from his own right wing. Those close to the Major talks say he failed to push the Unionists hard enough and ought to have been more flexible with the Nationalists who were beginning to acknowledge the futility of their terrorist campaign. New Labour took note of the reasons for Major's failed bid for peace. Early on, Blair took a particularly tough line with both sides, demanding agreement on power sharing by Good Friday of 1998. Martin McGuinness said in an interview in 2007:

> If he hadn't done that with the support of the Taoiseach, the entire project would have collapsed. I wasn't able to make an assessment of where Blair got his commitment from. Where did his intellectual and emotional engagement in the process come from? What powered him in all of this?[3]

What powered him was the thought of going down in history as the British prime minister who put an end to Northern Ireland's sectarian violence where all others had failed. But the added impetus that provided the 'emotional engagement' referred to by McGuinness, was the memory of Blair's Irish mother Hazel who died in her fifties from thyroid cancer. Bringing peace to Northern Ireland was political and personal, in part a tribute to the mother he had loved and lost when still a young man.

Blair's father Leo was a non-believer, so it was left to Hazel to be the driver of the children's early religious upbringing. She was a quiet, determined woman who lived for the family. For three years, the teenage Blair watched her patiently nursing Leo back to health after he suffered a stroke in 1964. In time, she taught him to speak again, but just as he was recovering, Blair's sister Sarah was diagnosed with Still's disease, a form of rheumatoid arthritis that took two years to bring under control. These were difficult times for the Blairs, but Hazel kept the family together, reassuring them constantly that 'everything would be all right' and encouraging both sons to work hard at school. 'Ten out of ten and nothing less' she would tell them. Ambitious for the family, she was delighted and proud when her elder son Bill, then Tony, won highly prized places to read Law at Oxford.

Hazel was diagnosed with cancer while Blair was at boarding school. Her condition stabilized after treatment but became much worse during Blair's final year at Oxford. Returning to Durham in 1975, he discovered that the worst had been kept from him for fear of disrupting his final exams. Leo met him at Durham Station. Blair's first question was, 'Is she going die?' 'Yes, she is' said his father quietly. She lived just a few more days.

It was a devastating blow to the young graduate, coming at a time when he was grappling with the question of what to do with the rest of his life. 'For the first time I felt not so much a sense of ambition as a consciousness that time is short. My life took on an urgency which has probably never left it.'[4]

To mark Blair's fiftieth birthday in April 2003, his brother Bill gave his only press interview to the *Observer* and said people had underestimated the role that Hazel had played in his brother's life.

The effect of our father's stroke on Tony has been analysed. I know many people say that the ambition of the father was transferred to the son. I think it is more complicated than that. The family picked itself up, as families do. I wouldn't want to give the impression that the following years were unhappy. They certainly were not. But five or six years later, my mother was diagnosed as having cancer of the thyroid. She died five years later. From Tony's perspective, I believe it was a combination of things that gave him the drive to succeed. The death of his mother affected him every bit as his father's stroke.[5]

Little is known about Hazel, other than she came from a staunchly Protestant family born in the flat above her grandmother Sally's hardware shop on the main street of Ballyshannon in Donegal. Sally's first husband, George Corscaden, came from a family of Protestant County Donegal farmers, descended from Scottish settlers who took their name from Garscadden, now part of Glasgow. George and Sally moved to Scotland in 1916 for a short period but returned to Northern Ireland. George died in 1923 when Hazel was a baby, and Sally remarried William McLay, a butcher, who moved the family back to Glasgow. Nor is much known about Sally except for her much-quoted advice to grandson, Tony, just before her death. 'Whatever you do, don't marry a Catholic', she warned.

The family kept their links with Northern Ireland. As a young boy, Blair would spend summer holidays in Rossnowlagh, the next village to Hazel's home town. They were idyllic times, free from school and teachers and work, interrupted only when the Troubles took hold of the province in the late 1960s.

Blair was the first British Prime Minister to address the Irish Parliament, and recalled: 'It was there in the seas off the Irish coast that I learnt to swim, there that my father took me to my first pub, a remote little house in the country, for a Guinness, a taste I've never forgotten and which is always a pleasure to repeat.'[6]

One of Blair's regrets is that his mother did not live to witness his remarkable political career. Northern Ireland entered his soul. 'It's in my blood', he told Irish MPs in 1998. Observers of the Northern Ireland negotiations are keen to tell of the hundreds of hours of gruelling talks, sometimes over several days, that would finally lead to a negotiated settlement and peace in the province. It was an inspired mission: Blair attacked it with a doggedness and dedication that has secured him a place in the history books. It was also the ultimate tribute to Hazel Blair.

Alastair Campbell noted in his diaries that at the end of his second week at Number 10, Northern Ireland was already one of Blair's top priorities. 'TB said he reckoned he could see a way of sorting the Northern Ireland problem. I loved the way he said it, like nobody had thought of it before. I said what makes you think you can do it when nobody else could?'[7]

There is no record of Blair's reply, but his presumed silence registered a resolve to bring an end to Northern Ireland's folly. Blair flew to Belfast on Friday 16 May, just two weeks after the election, with the immediate aim of persuading Sinn Fein to work towards a ceasefire. 'We only have a brief window of opportunity and we have to take it', he said.

The 'brief window of opportunity' was to dominate the next ten years of his premiership, ending triumphantly just days before his resignation, a fairy-tale ending after months of criticism over the Iraq war. How did he do it? How did he pull off a peace settlement that was beyond the wit of Gladstone and John Major and every holder of prime ministerial office in between?

Blair invested hundreds of hours and masses of energy, even through the dark days of Iraq, to finding a solution, and involved himself in the minutiae of day-to-day talks: 'You have to pay attention to the detail and commit one hundred per cent. You have to go right into the depths of it and you have to understand that if the two sides had been able to solve it themselves, they would have done it.'[8] The strategy was simple: persuading both sides that peace, through compromise, was possible if they would only give it a chance. Whenever negotiations hit a brick wall, Blair remained calm and reassuring. 'There's no point being angry. We just have to work out where to go from here.' At every juncture Blair, and his Chief of Staff Jonathan Powell, emphasized consent and made it clear that Labour's previous traditional support for a united Ireland was neutral under New Labour. He believed that there had been a sizeable shift in Republican thinking and, importantly, that the IRA craved to be taken seriously as a political force and sit around a negotiating table without ill-will. In time, could they be persuaded to postpone their call for Irish unification? 'The settlement train is leaving' was one of Blair's most over-used metaphors, but it got home the message; swap violence for politics, be with us or against us, or be it on your own heads.

By the following year, a negotiating team, chaired by the former American senator George Mitchell, whom Bill Clinton appointed special envoy to Northern Ireland, set a deadline.

Good Friday, 10 April 1998, was the date by which plans for devolved government in Northern Ireland had to be agreed in principle which included the early release of prisoners and the decommissioning of paramilitary weapons. Blair spent three days ensconced in Castle Buildings in the grounds of Stormont armed with the full set of advocacy skills he had once put to good use as a lawyer. Despite setbacks and hours of micro-managed negotiations, talks that wobbled were kept alive. Consensus won the day. The Good Friday Agreement offered a power-sharing assembly in Belfast that gave Northern Ireland self-rule within the United Kingdom, gave the Catholic community greater civil rights and reform, while the Irish Government agreed to withdraw its territorial claim on the north. Blair called it 'the hands of history' and was applauded worldwide for the momentous breakthrough. For the first time, Unionists accepted they would have to share power, while the IRA had to contemplate the idea of decommissioning their arsenal of weapons (which was to take the next ten years to achieve). Blair told the Irish Parliament: 'It's all about belonging. The wish of the unionists is to belong to the UK. The wish of the nationalists is to belong to Ireland. Both traditions are reasonable. There are no absolutes. The beginning of understanding is to realize that.'[9]

Yet years of mistrust and hatred ran deep. It was going to take more than a document, no matter how historic, to stem fears on both sides. Six weeks after the Good Friday Agreement was signed, the people of the north and south in separate referendums endorsed it. But the extreme Democratic Unionist Party, led by Ian Paisley, refused to accept that the

Nationalists could ever have parity in the province. He called Blair a 'liar' who had sold out to the Republicans. For their part, Gerry Adams and Martin McGuinness saw the Good Friday Agreement as the first step to peace. For them, there was no going back.

JB: *It was all going so well, but there was always the danger that some sort of incident would scupper the negotiations. Tony had put so much into it. He kept it going when not many people believed it could ever have a successful outcome. There's a fund of stories about the negotiations and the brinkmanship, one side coming on board, the other taking umbrage, the need to believe a settlement was possible. I remember him telling me about one meeting just before the final agreement was reached. The talks had gone on for hours without any real progress being made, and he always believed that one of the most important things was to keep the group together, keep them talking. Suddenly one bloke took offence at something or other, jumped up and announced he'd had enough. He was leaving. Apparently Tony jumped to his feet and got to the door before him, blocking it with his outstretched arms. He said he looked at the guy's face and suddenly realized he hadn't a clue what he was going to say to him to persuade him to stay. I think the guy was so astonished at the British Prime Minister's splayed arms that he huffed and puffed and meekly sat down again.*

A few months later, of course, the car bomb in Omagh happened and everyone held their breath. It was a tragedy of the worst kind, 29 innocent people killed, and there was a real danger that the outrage would completely kill off the peace process. But it seemed to have the opposite effect. Republicans were as horrified as the rest of the world at the carnage and, if anything, instead of knocking the peace negotiations off track, it helped to strengthen the case for peace.

The Good Friday Agreement was a significant breakthrough although a fragile pact; up to the eleventh hour, the prospect of a final deal on power sharing was always in doubt. The Assembly was suspended, returned to power and suspended again as arguments raged, among other issues, about the fate of IRA weapons. In 2000, power was formally devolved from Westminster, then reinstated ten weeks later. The deadline set by the Good Friday Agreement was 22 May 2000. There were two major objectives, devolved government and decommissioning of weapons. The deadline was missed but two weeks later both sides accepted the conditions and power sharing was restored, this time without the Good Friday fanfare. A month later, on 30 June 2000 at Tübingen University in Germany, Blair addressed a meeting of the Global Ethics Foundation and reminded the world that the history of Northern Ireland taught us that ancient divisions can be healed:

There are those who reject change, people who believe that if you don't fit in with their view of the world, you don't belong. But they are in the minority. The majority rejected the old ways. They voted for change. For the first time ever, Northern Ireland has an inclusive government voted for by the people of Northern Ireland.

I am proud of what has been achieved in Northern

Ireland. I am honoured by the interest shown in it around the world. With the support and prayers of millions outside Northern Ireland, I know we can build a future of peace and harmony in Northern Ireland. But what is the fundamental lesson of Northern Ireland for us all? For me it is this. There is no place in the twenty-first century for narrow and exclusive traditions. It underlines the supreme importance in the modern world of understanding our dependence on one another, for future progress.[10]

Privately, Blair feared for the fragility of the peace process. Alastair Campbell in his diaries wrote:

TB was worried it was all going down the pan again. Bertie (Ahern) was equally gloomy. The date of an IRA statement and lack of certainty about decommissioning were holding us back. TB was exasperated that they could not grasp the fact that they were about to deliver the death of the IRA if only they would seize it.[11]

Gerry Adams had been the first of the Irish leaders to broaden his analysis of party issues and, in the 1980s, had held a number of secret meetings with politicians of all sides. By the 1990s, his efforts resulted in an IRA ceasefire when Republicans agreed to test the proposition that violence could be replaced by political dialogue and votes could prove more effective than guns. In the process, the death rate fell, heralding a semblance of normality returning to Belfast. The benefits were clear to Sinn Fein, more so when their share of the vote increased dramatically and Sinn Fein became Northern Ireland's largest nationalist party. For all that, they still had some way to go to prove their genuine commitment to peace, with the litmus test of Republican authority being the thorny question of decommissioning and bringing an end to criminality.

For Blair, there was the greater challenge of negotiating with the stubborn, fiery Ian Paisley, a flamboyant fundamentalist preacher who had flaunted his anti-Catholic feelings over the years. Paisley boycotted the peace negotiations, calling them an IRA plot. He condemned the Pope and the Catholic Church as 'the whore of Babylon', accused the Irish Government of 75 years of systematic ethnic cleansing of Protestants, and there was the constant spectre of an avenging God ready to strike down Paisley's enemies. And as late as February 2006, at the DUP's annual conference, he launched a blistering attack on Blair, accusing him of 'encouraging IRA criminality' because of the British Government's decision to give Sinn Fein more money from the public purse. How did the relationship move from open hostility to a close friendship?

In March 2007, Ian Paisley confirmed to the *Guardian* newspaper that, in time, discussions with the Prime Minister had gone far beyond politics. Paisley agreed that he began to believe he could do business with Blair when he became convinced his faith was genuine. Asked whether he shared an interest in religion with the Prime Minister, he said: 'We shared religious books that I thought would be good for him to read, and I'm sure he read them. He always takes books away with him.'[12] In one interview, Paisley said the assorted theological tracts seemed to give comfort to 'a very troubled spirit'.

It was a two-way process. According to Anthony Seldon:

> Blair focused on Paisley, carving out quality time to talk to him one-on-one. He steered their conversation onto almost any subject other than Northern Ireland and slowly Paisley grew to like him and trust him, a development helped by the 'very respectful' view he held of the Prime Minister of the United Kingdom. An idea lodged in his mind that he 'did not want to disappoint the Prime Minister and to do a deal if he possibly could'.[13]

Was Paisley's about-turn a reflection of his friendship with Blair? Did he see it as the last-ditch attempt for peace in Northern Ireland? Was it the only way he could rid the province of the IRA? Did his brush with his Maker in 2004, when he was said to be near death's door, bring about a change of heart and a desire for peace?

It was an amalgam of all these things and, cynics would say, the promise of the top job in a power-sharing government. However, Paisley's final push for peace was hindered by a number of Free Presbyterian ministers who waged theological warfare, urging Paisley to reject the peace deal. One senior cleric accused him of 'abandoning a truly biblical position regarding murderers in government'. But Paisley hit back using his trademark hyperbole. In a church newsletter, he accused his critics of slandering God's leadership, warning

'It is the ploy of Satan to attack those whom God has appointed and specially anointed as leaders in his work.'[14]

One serious error of judgement on Blair's part was to assume that the fragile peace would strengthen the moderate parties of left and right. It had the reverse effect. The SDLP and the Ulster Unionists were abandoned for Sinn Fein and Democratic Unionists who became the two largest parties in the province and made the final agreement even more remarkable as extreme Nationalist and Republican demands were put to one side and their signatures added to the final power-sharing document. Who could have imagined pictures of Ian Paisley and Gerry Adams – the ex-IRA commander and the Ulster demagogue – sitting shoulder to shoulder, pledging their undying willingness to work together? It would have been beyond belief in 1997 – more so by the two men themselves – to have even contemplated any form of peaceful co-existence. Yet the most unlikely pairing in history came together unapologetically, with the two warriors exuding a sense of purpose, declaring that the war was over and offering firm promises to run Northern Ireland together for the good of all the people, whatever their religious creeds.

Peace in Northern Ireland was a victory for Blair's political agility and intelligent handling of both Catholic and Protestant (described by one official as his 'constructive ambiguity'). His ability to straddle the religious divide in his personal life – a high Anglican at the time who regularly attended Mass with his Catholic family – stood him in good stead in his dealings with Sinn Fein and the Democratic Unionist Party. The working relationship with Sinn Fein leaders,

Adams and McGuinness, while never easy, was businesslike, although it led to protests from Conservative politicians who thought it abhorrent to be holding any level of discussions with key figures of the Republican movement. Yet failing to engage the Nationalists had been Major's fatal mistake. Blair had no intention of repeating it, insisting on talking with members of all political parties, no matter what their past criminal records might show and no matter how vehemently some MPs shouted their protests at Westminster.

With a deal tantalizingly near, Paisley feared he might be unable to take the Party with him, a fear he shared with the Prime Minister on 26 March 2007, just weeks before the final deadline. The Republicans also worried that Paisley would fail to deliver and for their part worried that Adams, too, might fail to persuade his Sinn Fein colleagues to take the path to decommissioning.

The added spur to finding a solution was the generally accepted view that Blair's tenure at Number 10 was coming to an end. Adams was dismayed at the thought of having to deal with a new Prime Minister who might not be as focused on finding a solution as Blair. Moreover, Adams and McGuinness were known to be comfortable with his style and neutrality.

JB: *During the Christmas period just before he stood down, Tony and Jonathan Powell were constantly on the phone to both sides, pushing for concessions, determined not to let progress slip. And to see it come together just days before Tony resigned was the pinnacle, listening to Paisley and McGuinness committing to non-violence and peaceful means, a dream beyond measure.*

119

Ahern said afterwards that Blair had been a true friend of Ireland and he certainly was – not only because of the time and effort that had gone in to finding a peace formula, but because the situation in Northern Ireland was one of the main reasons why Tony stood back from converting to the Catholic Church. I suppose the DUP might have taken a very dim view of negotiating with a Catholic prime minister – even though Ian Paisley was eventually very much on side and there was a warm friendship and respect between the two men.

But peace in Northern Ireland removed the final obstacle to Tony's decision to become a Catholic. After that, it was a certainty. It makes you wonder what his mother would have made of the Northern Ireland deal – her son bringing peace to her beloved place of birth. He never talked much about her, but wouldn't she have been proud? What a tribute.

In an interview in the *Guardian* in March 2007, Martin McGuinness said in the many hours of talks with Blair, he never once mentioned his Irish mother. 'He probably thought we would have railed against her being a Protestant, not that it would have mattered one jot what she was. Donegal Protestants are good people, just like Protestants all over Ireland are very good people.' A decade ago, the comment would have been as unlikely as Paisley's eventual enthusiastic praise of power sharing, the same Paisley who declared a few years earlier that true Protestants would not be fooled by the 'double speak of the Hail Mary brigade of Anglican Ecumenists'. But the vitriolic language that had inflamed the Irish Question for decades in the name of religion was put to one side, along with the bombs and the guns and the despair.

At the historic meeting between Paisley and Adams on 27 March, witnessed by an astonished press core, Paisley's language was conciliatory, mutual respect was to the fore, as he announced the date for devolution, adding: 'We must not allow our justified loathing of the horrors and tragedies of the past to become a barrier to creating a better and more stable future.'[15]

The war was over, the violence tamed, the people had made it clear it was time to pull back from the dark side of religion into the realms of a moderate Christianity for the sake of both communities. This was a new era. The Troubles were over. Real political debate could begin, underpinning the peace process with sound policies for the benefit of Catholic and Protestant alike.

Blair said after the signing ceremony on 8 May 2007: 'Look back and we see centuries marked by conflict, hardship, even hatred among the people of these islands: look forward and see the chance to shake off the heavy chains of history.'[16] The heavy chains of history have been cast aside. In the past few years, Northern Ireland has been transformed. The economy is back on track. Lives have been saved, and although still plagued by pockets of sectarianism, the hunger for peace is as strong as ever. A decade after the Good Friday Agreement, it seems inconceivable that the people of Northern Ireland will ever again allow their island to be sucked back into the cruel and desperate 'time of the Troubles'. It is Blair's legacy, and Hazel Blair would have awarded her Prime Minister son ten out of ten for his efforts.

In an emotional resignation speech back in his Sedgefield constituency on 10 May 2007, just two days after the historic Northern Ireland accord was signed, Blair talked of the agonies of the decision-making process. 'People think you act with messianic zeal. Doubt, hesitation, reflection, consideration and reconsideration – these are all good companions of proper decision-making. But the ultimate obligation is to decide.'[17]

Nothing could shake Blair's belief that religious dialogue and understanding were essential to peace because 'ignorance creates fear which creates conflict'. Moreover, faith and moral values played a central role in Blair's decision-making that became even more apparent when dealing with evil dictators and the abuse of human rights. With God on his side, and tried and tested negotiating skills put to good use in Kosovo, Sierra Leone and Northern Ireland, Blair began to believe he was unassailable, with his determination, patience and an impressive track record leading to dialogue, compromise and inclusivity, the ingredients of successful negotiations. Were these skills transferable to other troubled nations?

Kosovo and Sierra Leone had benefited greatly from Blair's commitment to intervening in the affairs of those nations which abused and oppressed their own people. Afghanistan, and of course Iraq, were to prove more complex, but this only boosted Blair's resolve to stand firm against Saddam's brutality and the threat, he believed, the dictator posed to world peace.

CHAPTER 7

Striding the International Stage

Hope has two beautiful daughters. Their names are anger and courage; anger at the way things are, and courage to see that they do not remain the way they are.[1]

So what to make of a Prime Minister who, during his ten years in power, confessed to disliking both Westminster and Whitehall? Westminster was a talking shop, he would say privately, while Whitehall was painfully obstructive. Members of Parliament and civil servants apart, there was also the bullying Scot at Number 11 who was becoming increasingly contrary as the Government's first term neared its end. Although Blair's political nous told him that he needed to get to grips with New Labour's core aims – fighting poverty and improving schools and hospitals – his frustration with the slow, grinding mechanism of government, and ongoing battles with Brown, made life on the political home front irksome. Climbing aboard a plane, any plane, seemed preferable to the political battering-ram at home.

Therein lies a grain of truth, although Blair's preference for matters foreign was more complex than a yearning to escape Whitehall, Westminster and Gordon Brown. Those close to him say he was driven by a sense of Gladstonian moralism, a latter-day St Michael's angel fighting the might of Lucifer, emboldened by values that were more clearly defined on foreign soil: iniquitous ethnic cleansing in Eastern Europe, addressing corruption and poverty in Africa, and the worsening situation in the Middle East, all the while adopting a supreme confidence that led him to believe he could shoulder deep-seated international crises that had defeated world leaders for decades.

This was Blair's moral crusade which was unrelated to a personal God, linked instead to his belief that 'being Christian' was about engaging and nurturing community. But this was no cosy, domestic ideology restricted to the home front. From it arose the doctrine of international community, the justification for humanitarian intervention in the affairs of other nation states, a variation on the theme of the parable of the people and talents that reminded those countries with power to take responsibility for the poor and oppressed. In a seminal speech in Chicago in 1999 that became a noted text for political analysts and academics, Blair explained the thinking behind 'the doctrine of international community'.

> By this I mean the explicit recognition that today, more than ever, we are mutually dependent, that national interest is to a significant extent governed by international collaboration and that we need a clear and coherent debate as to the direction this doctrine takes us in each

field of international endeavour. Just as within domestic politics the notion of community – the belief that partnership and co-operation are essential to advance self-interest – is coming into its own, so it needs to find its own international echo.[2]

The Chicago speech expounded Blair's foreign policy mindset. Outlining what became known as the 'Blair Doctrine', he called for a re-examination of the traditional notions of national sovereignty for the twenty-first century and suggested five criteria to be established whenever military intervention was under consideration. Are we sure of our case? Have we exhausted all diplomatic options? Can the military operation be prudently undertaken? Is there a will to hold out for the long term if required? Are there national interests involved? It was the sharp end of 'international community', a rationale for exhorting universal freedoms, ending tyranny and rewarding the people with democratic government. If not setting the international agenda, Blair was clarifying it and, soon after taking power, acting upon it.

In 1998, British warplanes joined the American bombing of Iraq in 'Operation Desert Fox'. This was good fighting evil, protecting the weak, ousting the enemy and if necessary by force. Four days of bombing Iraqi military installations hardly raised an eyebrow back home, although Blair came under fire from Nelson Mandela. The Prime Minister defended his position: 'When the international community agrees on certain objectives, and then fails to implement them, those that can act, must.'[3]

It was a significant departure from non-interventionism that had restrained European leaders since the Second World War. Yet how could the leader of the British Labour Party, a party traditionally anti-American and anti-war, engage in, and in many respects lead the West's rallying call to war?

There were several reasons. In 1998, Blair was seen as a political phenomenon in Europe and America, 'a breath of fresh air', a politician for the twenty-first century; in part, too, his call for nations to intervene was strengthened by the sheer scale of New Labour's parliamentary majority that made it tricky for the left to make its voice heard; the Good Friday Agreement in Northern Ireland was a considerable morale and confidence booster that had won worldwide respect. All the while his message at home and abroad was consistent: Britain must become part of a worldwide peace and harmony initiative guided by mutual self-interest and moral purpose.

'If we can establish and spread the values of liberty, the rule of law, human rights and an open society, then that is in our national interests too. The spread of our values makes us safer', Blair told the Chicago audience. John F. Kennedy put it more succinctly: 'Freedom is indivisible, and when one man is enslaved, who is free?'[4]

If 'Operation Desert Fox' was the prologue to Blair's foreign policy, Kosovo was the first act (the final act would be played out in Iraq). In March 1999, the international community applauded as Blair rallied support to defend the Muslim people of the Balkans. The situation in Kosovo was rapidly deteriorating. Human rights abuses were commonplace under President Slobodan Milosevic. Serb forces had turned on the country's Muslim majority with relentless savagery. Refugees were forced out of their homes, pouring onto the streets and into makeshift camps. Television pictures captured the horror of 25,000 people trudging the highways, beaten and battered by Serbian soldiers. The world was stunned into inaction. Blair was acutely aware of the sensitivities within the Party of waging war but he reminded members that intervention in Rwanda five years earlier would have prevented the slaughter of a million people, 'a scar on the conscience of the world'. He asked, 'Would the free world once again stand aside and do nothing? Acts of genocide could never be an internal matter.'

Claiming that it was 'the right thing to do', he steamrollered the call for troop deployment through the House of Commons, telling members, 'To walk away now would be a breach of faith with thousands of innocent civilians whose only desire is to live in peace and who took us at our word.'[5]

In the same month, NATO announced that it was preparing a military response after several attempts to put diplomatic pressure on Milosevic had failed. But could NATO adapt from being a defensive to an attacking force? Of the 19 NATO countries, Greece and Italy had already announced they were opposed to any form of military intervention, and despite NATO's threat to respond militarily, Milosevic remained impervious to NATO threats, confident there would be no consensus among member countries for an all-out attack. He was right. Predictably the Russians vetoed any endorsement for air strikes at the UN Security Council and

Milosevic was left to carry on pursuing his barbarous ethnic cleansing acts. Kosovo was another Rwanda in the making, and the Russian veto should not be allowed to hinder military intervention: Blair warned that the reality rather than the threat of force was the only way forward.

The first air attack took place at 8pm local time on 24 March in the somewhat naïve belief that 72 hours of intensive bombing would force Milosevic to the negotiating table, a wildly optimistic forecast. As the bombing continued throughout April, hundreds of innocent lives were lost and the refugee crisis worsened, with thousands of Kosovars uprooted, not as a consequence of ethnic cleansing but as a direct result of the bombing. Blair was desperate for some sign of a breakthrough, reminding a dubious public back home that Milosevic's regime was every bit as heinous as Hitler's regime: 'We have learnt twice before in this century that appeasement does not work. If we let an evil dictator rage unchallenged, we will have to spill infinitely more blood and treasure to stop him later.'[6] Despite the plea, support for the war was dwindling, and on 3 May, Blair and Cherie travelled to Stankovic in Macedonia to witness for themselves the plight of the refugees. The visit was a public relations exercise to muster support for the bombing. It was also Blair's first visit to a refugee camp, a visit that would strengthen his resolve to see the war through. 'This is not a battle for territory, this is a battle for humanity. It is a just cause' he told journalists later, backing his claim again with reference to the five criteria.

The following day, Blair addressed the Romanian Parliament, the first British Prime Minister to do so. It was an emotional speech that, somehow, received little media attention back home:

> Yesterday, I visited the Stankovic refugee camp. Thousands upon thousands of people, stoic and strong, but living an existence no person should be forced to endure. I visited the Blace border post. As far as the eye could see, a queue of humanity stretched through no-man's-land to Kosovo. Dignified in their pain and terror. Eyes glazed, mothers struggling to soothe children under a blistering sun. Old men staring vacantly into a new country and a future they could not predict. Slowly they were processed from one queue to the next. Their message was simple and it was dignified. We are leaving for now, but please, please help us to go back.
>
> I felt an anger so strong, a loathing of what Milosevic's policy stands for, so powerful that I pledged to them, as I pledge to you now: that Milosevic and his hideous racial genocide will be defeated. NATO will prevail. And the refugees will be allowed to return in safety to their homes.[7]

The speech was Blair's 'battle for humanity', the crux of his faith that extended beyond Christianity because 'Jews, Christians and Muslims were all children of God'. His reaction to Stankovic was Messianic. 'I pledge to you now, that Milosevic and his hideous racial genocide will be defeated.' This was Blair's rock-hard conviction at its most raw that militated against him listening to advisers like Sir Charles Guthrie, the

Government's military chief. Blair was coming to the view that, in order to defeat Milosevic, ground troops would have to be deployed. The bombs had rained down for 70 days and the loss of innocent life was escalating. The prudent Sir Charles cautioned him against the risk of the war escalating out of control and had reason to believe that the Americans would never commit to ground troops: intervention would only lead to failure and humiliation, he warned. Despite the prospect of losing public support, Blair listened and replied politely that Sir Charles should prepare troops for a ground war. It was the only answer. It was Milosevic's worst nightmare, a nightmare the Serb leader believed would never happen. And it was the turning point of the war.

Clinton had persistently resisted Blair's call for 'boots on the ground'. Nevertheless, on 27 May, George Robertson announced that 50,000 troops would be deployed to Kosovo. The pressure mounted and the Americans had little choice other than to announce that they, too, were on the point of pressing the button to deploy ground force troops. Finally, when the Russians informed Milosevic that they would do nothing to prevent a ground war, he agreed to withdraw his troops. On 10 June, the NATO Secretary-General suspended the bombing campaign. As a postscript to the Balkans operation, it is worth noting that as a consequence of the Russian veto, Britain failed to secure UN support for the bombing and not a single voice was raised in protest, presumably because the operation was deemed a success.

Blair's boldness, in not only challenging Milosevic but also challenging Clinton, boosted his standing further on the world stage, defined by many as the crisis that turned a fledgling Prime Minister into a crusading politician. In terms of the five criteria, the rationale for intervention in Kosovo had been adhered to, despite international pressure during the three-month bombing campaign. As Milosevic was forced to pull back and the Kosovars returned to their homes, the world became curious about the British Prime Minister whose missionary zeal had been fired by the belief that 'it was the right thing to do'. Moreover, his hawkish posture and tough moral stance contrasted sharply with an increasingly enfeebled American president who had become embroiled in the Monica Lewinsky scandal.

Politically, Blair was on a roll, although he knew that despite Clinton's prevarication, success in the Balkans had relied heavily on American support, without which the Kosovo story might have had a very different and tragic ending. But success in Kosovo, and ongoing progress in Northern Ireland, energized Blair and taught him a lesson about the folly of appeasement. It also cemented the notion that he was fast becoming the bridge between the US and Europe, claiming, for example, that international security had been significantly strengthened by the joint action taken by the UK and the US.

A year later, still fired by the Balkans campaign, Britain took the decision to send troops to Sierra Leone, a country paralysed by a bloody civil war where civilians were dependent upon a UN peacekeeping force on the verge of collapse. Rebel forces were dangerously close to taking the capital Freetown. Time was running out. Blair deployed British troops ostensibly to oversee the evacuation of foreign nationals but ordered them to stay on to support the Kabbah Government and help retrain Sierra Leone's army. The British presence helped stabilize the situation and led to the arrest of the rebel leader Foday Sankoh who was later tried for crimes against humanity. Blair's confidence was given a further boost, although while applauded abroad for his leadership, he received little praise at home. The Opposition continued calling for the withdrawal of troops while Blair replied that 'moral purpose and enlightened self-interest argued for more assertive intervention'.

Meanwhile, Britain's secular movement mounted a challenge to the wisdom and 'moral purpose' of Blair's foreign policy. They argued that he and other Western leaders defined interventionism as war against 'terror and evil' when in reality the 'so-called terrorists' were motivated, like Christians, by what their own religions deemed honourable. Were they not simply carrying out the commands of their spiritual mentors, no matter how misguided?

Blair's 'third way' mentor, Amitai Etzioni, put it this way:

Like Che Guevara put it, if you want to have an omelette you have to crack eggs, which means if you want to have a revolution you have to crack heads, and you find Fabians and people who would not kill a fly, and you find Jews on the West Bank, and you'll find peaceniks who want to turn over their last acre of land for peace. And you find the same thing in Christianity, you have the sword, or peace and turn the other cheek. And you find exactly the same thing in Islam.[8]

The argument was familiar to the Prime Minister but it cut little ice with a politician whose complex mix of charm and ruthlessness, courage and bellicosity, had marked him out as an international risk-taker. Having found a purpose difficult to match in workaday domestic politics, advisers, journalists and the party faithful asked, who had created Blair the Warrior? Where had he come from? Was he a saint, a martyr, a hero fighting the West's enemies? Or was he the politician-actor seeking a world stage for his own self-aggrandisement? The public and press started looking for smoke and mirrors, Blair the moralist who set out his political stall according to the writings of an obscure Scottish philosopher and pacifist John Macmurray, hailed as an international statesman abroad and regarded with suspicion at home.

JB: *This was when the job became relentless, and yet the biggest challenge, Iraq, was yet to come. Kosovo, particularly, gave him more confidence because he was not only standing up to military advisers, he was also standing up to the American president. Yes, he had the common touch but his real strength was that he could follow through an argument to the bitter end without ever losing sight of the detail. He believed that if it was possible to do something about injustice, then you should do it – which is why it's very simple to explain the idea of Blair the Warrior. It was part of Tony living out his faith. Even so, the pressures were huge. He was on top of the job and trusted his own instincts, convinced that sending in ground troops was the only way to put an end to the despicable regime there. But the stakes were high. Tony was out on a limb. He came through it, but the end result was never certain. Then people* *started questioning why he wasn't applying the same principle more widely, that if a moral code applied to one country then it should be applied elsewhere. What about Darfur, Zimbabwe, Burma? I say 'relentless' because if he could have done something about regime change in those countries, he would have done. Then 9/11 happened and everything changed.*

Millions of viewers watched in horror at television pictures from New York when two commercial planes crashed into the North and South Towers of the World Trade Center. Forty minutes went by before a third plane crashed into the south-west corner of the Pentagon. Unbelievably, the United States of America was under attack. Blair was quick to grasp that nothing would ever be the same again between the super-power and the rest of the world. After the shock waves and the outpouring of grief came the call to seek out the perpetrators. Blair's first thought was to persuade Bush that despite the tragedy, America must seek a multilateral response. At the same time, he impressed on the American President that Britain would stand 'shoulder to shoulder' in their efforts to defeat Al Qaeda and the Taliban. Bush agreed that the priority was Afghanistan but ominously noted that he would come back to Iraq in due course.

A month after 9/11, Blair delivered a powerful address to the Labour Party Conference and paid tribute to those who had lost their lives, reminding the civilized world that the response was not just about punishing the guilty:

It is that out of the shadow of this evil should emerge lasting good; destruction of the machinery of terrorism wherever it is found; hope amongst all nations of a new beginning where we seek to resolve our differences in a calm and ordered way; greater understanding between nations and between faiths, and above all justice and prosperity for the poor and dispossessed, so that people everywhere can see a chance of a better future through hard work and creative power of the free citizen, not the violence and savagery of the fanatic.[9]

He concluded, 'I have long since believed that this interdependence defines the new world we live in.' The moral tone took flight, overtaking the realities of fighting global terrorism. 'Out of the shadow of evil should emerge lasting good.' 'A battle for justice and prosperity for the poor and dispossessed.' Were they the words of a politician or a priest? Where were the boundaries? British commentators thought the speech too preachy, while the American press reported that it was Blair's bid for world leadership. The Prime Minister believed he had sought and found the language to present a moral case for war, and in those nervous post-9/11 days, the majority applauded his endeavours.

While Osama Bin Laden remained at large, the military campaign in Afghanistan completed the task of destroying an important sanctuary for the Taliban. But the question remained hanging in the air: would Britain join the United States in any planned invasion of Iraq? The Bush administration was described as a juggernaut hurtling along, out of control. The question was whether Britain would climb on board.

JB: *There was almost an inevitability about Britain joining the American effort. Tony had made it very clear that he would stand by them. It was also true that his experience in Kosovo, Sierra Leone and Northern Ireland had given him a voice abroad that was being listened to. I was nervous about it and nervous for him. I remember saying to him that it would be easier to do nothing. Actually, he looked a little hurt and said 'easy' wasn't an option. Remember, he was surrounded by masses of intelligence, not only from America and the UK, but, what people didn't realize, it was also coming from French and Russian intelligence services. It was also Tony's view that Bush shouldn't be allowed to go it alone. He was desperate to get it right but frustrated with the response at home, saying several times how he couldn't win the argument because he was constantly criticized over his relationship with Bush and yet the world was urging him to be a restraining influence. How could he influence Bush at a distance? Bush would have gone straight in, let's not forget that, and Tony rightly stayed close to the President, which is one of the reasons why the Americans respected him so much. The body blow was when Chirac announced that he wouldn't support a second UN resolution in any circumstances. It seemed obvious to most people that it was an anti-Blair decision. Chirac didn't like the fact that Tony had become Mr Europe. Yes, it was a difficult time. I didn't see much of him then. He was flying round the world at a crazy pace. When I did see him, you could see him visibly ageing.*

I suppose it's easy to look back and say that if it wasn't for Iraq,

Tony would still be Prime Minister today, but you can't do that. A crisis comes along and decisions have to be taken, and whatever you think of his policies, he's never shirked from taking decisions. So he went from country to country repeating the same message: if we don't deal with Iraq now, it'll become a much bigger job in the years to come. In any event, despite pleading with Bush to go to the UN for support and his genuine concern about the dangers of weapons of mass destruction, the war was always going to happen. Bush had made up his mind, with or without us.

The twists and turns of the Iraq war have been debated else-where at great length. But before moving into the dark shadow of war that cast a cloud over a promising premiership – the invasion of Iraq was the beginning of the end of Blair's popularity at home – what part did religion play in his increasingly bellicose behaviour? Blair's abiding plea – if you can act, then do it – meant there was little alternative other than offering to support Bush, but his endorsement of the American invasion was never hollow support. The Prime Minister was 100 per cent behind Bush's plan to remove Saddam and with him the threat of weapons of mass destruction that he believed existed. Blair was in no doubt of Britain's obligations, but more than that of his personal obligation as a Christian. He would scratch his head in bewilderment, asking how the left could possibly oppose the removal of a dictator who was guilty of genocide and had used chemical weapons against his own people. Surely no kingdom has had as many wars as the kingdom of Christ, said anti-war campaigners. While Blair's response was instinctive, church leaders remained cautious.

For centuries the Catholic Church had taken the view that a 'just war' was acceptable under certain conditions. St Augustine, in the fourth century, set out three provisos: war must occur for a good and just purpose rather than for self-gain or an exercise of power; 'just war' must be waged by a properly instituted authority, such as the state; love must be the central motive even in the midst of violence. 'Just war' theorists also insisted that the use of arms must be restrained, made more humane and directed towards establishing lasting peace and justice and always asking the questions: when is it right to resort to armed force (*jus ad bellum*) and what is acceptable in using such force (*jus in bello*)? More recently a third category was added, addressing the end of war, peace agreements and the position of war criminals (*jus post bellum*). In the name of Augustine, Catholic leaders acknowledged that war could be justified if certain conditions were met.

In the months before the Iraqi invasion, the question raged over whether it constituted a 'just war' but predictably those on both sides of the argument interpreted the theory to suit their cause. Supporters believed that the enforcement of UN resolutions was sufficient authority for a 'just war'. Opponents insisted that a 'just war' required a specific Security Council resolution and, moreover, the criteria for 'just war' were so artful and open to manipulation that all politicians could claim their war 'just'. Moreover, if the invasion was believed to be 'just', extreme moral absolutism could well dictate the conduct of war that would make excessive military force acceptable.

The almost universal belief of religious leaders was that the invasion of Iraq did not meet the criteria of a 'just war'. Pope John Paul was adamant that invading Iraq could not be justified either morally or legally, that war was a defeat for humanity. There was papal criticism, too, for the most powerful nations at the UN Security Council which were said to be exerting pressure on the less powerful nations.

When war, as in these days in Iraq, threatens the fate of humanity, it is ever more urgent to proclaim, with a strong and decisive voice, that only peace is the road to follow to construct a more just and united society. Violence and arms can never resolve the problems of man.[10]

The Pope spoke out against the planned invasion almost daily and sent his personal representative, Cardinal Pio Laghi, a friend of the Bush family, to remonstrate with the US President, insisting that the war would be illegal and unjust. The message was clear: God is not on your side if you invade.

Blair chose to ignore the Pope's intercession and dismissed the advice of other senior church leaders. It was better to act than do nothing, he would reply, even though the outcome was uncertain, a view supporters say showed courage and conviction while opponents called it cowboy politics, hubristic and stubborn. He was dubbed a Manichee, seeing only light and darkness. Others called him Antinomian – what he does is right by virtue of the fact that he does it.

No one could persuade Blair otherwise. Seeking refuge in the 'just war' argument, he offered support to the US while stipulating three conditions that were Augustinian in substance: an effort must be made to assemble the largest possible coalition against Saddam, there must be a commitment to working through the United Nations, and planning for war must be made in tandem with a road map for Middle East peace. According to Sir Christopher Meyer, however, Blair was a true believer in the threat of Saddam Hussein and had 'an instinctive and immediate sympathy for what George Bush was planning to do'.[11]

And so Blair set out on a frenetic diplomatic effort to boost support for the American invasion, to find a 'coalition of the willing' despite the real possibility that his pro-war stance could cost him the premiership. Had he lost the crucial House of Commons vote on 18 March 2003, he would have had no alternative other than to offer his resignation. Nor was he pink-faced at the outcome of the vote, a majority on the back of Conservative support. Around one-third of the Parliamentary Labour Party rebelled, but it was enough for his survival that he carried the support of more than half the Party.

'Trust Tony's judgement' won the day, a judgement based on an implicit Christian belief that Britain should confront tyranny wherever possible – with the caveat of enlightened self-interest. The Pope may say otherwise, but Blair repeated, time and again, in high moral tones that often jarred with the stink of war: 'It was the right thing to do.' The mountain of evidence that weapons of mass destruction existed could not be ignored, nor should Saddam be allowed to carry out his murderous acts of genocide against his own people. The

Tony, Cherie and Euan Blair, outside 'Myrobella', 1984.

Kitchen politics: Tony Blair and John Burton at 'Myrobella', 1996.

'Myrobella' memoir! John Burton and Tony Blair.

Tony Blair and John Burton at Newbiggin in Northumberland, May 1996.

The new Prime Minister and Cherie Blair with John and Lily Burton, 1997.

Second time lucky. June 2001.

world of interdependent communities demanded action and it would be unchristian, inhumane and negligent to walk away.

What of Blair's three conditions for backing the Americans? On the question of amassing 'the largest possible coalition', Blair's support for hostilities encouraged other countries, which were originally against the planned invasion, to offer troops; but it was a modest coalition including Spain, Australia, the Netherlands and Poland. On the second count, Blair fought to the end to win a second resolution and failed, despite being assured that the war was legal under Resolution 1441. And George Bush was persuaded to keep the Middle East peace process alive, although the Bush Administration gave it only sporadic attention.

On 20 March 2003 at 5.33am local time, the first explosion was heard in Baghdad. As the invasion got under way, Blair was called upon to justify his action. Looking grey and drawn, he addressed the nation:

> Some say if we act, we become a target. The truth is, all nations are targets. Bali was never in the front line of action against terrorism. America didn't attack Al Qaeda. They attacked America. Britain has never been a nation to hide at the back. But even if we were, it wouldn't avail us. Should terrorists obtain these weapons now being manufactured and traded round the world, the carnage they could inflict on our economies, our security, to world peace, would be beyond our most vivid imagination. That is why I have asked British troops to go into action tonight.

A year after the invasion, Blair continued to justify the decision and, like a wounded animal, returned to his home patch to lick his wounds. In a speech, in his Sedgefield constituency on 5 March 2004, warning of the continued threat of global terrorism, Blair defended his decision in an emotional outpouring. Acknowledging that the Government needed to focus on domestic issues – on pledges that had made New Labour's election triumphs possible – he said the nature of the situation in Iraq could not be swept away. Taking on board personal criticism:

> It is the task of leadership to expose it (the global threat) and fight it, whatever the political cost; and the true danger is not to any single politician's reputation but to our country if we ignore this threat or erase it from the agenda in embarrassment at the difficulties it causes.[12]

This was classic Blair, obliquely reminding the world that the threat was real and existential and, in accepting shared responsibility for the invasion, he had put his reputation and career on the line. In a detailed analysis of the rationale that led to war, and defending his integrity in the process, he spoke of the overwhelming global intelligence that led him to believe that Saddam and leaders of other rogue states saw weapons of mass destruction as a means of defending themselves. And he was concerned on two other fronts:

> The first was the increasing amount of information about Islamic extremism and terrorism that was crossing my desk.

Chechnya was blighted by it. So was Kashmir. Afghanistan was its training ground. The extremism seemed remarkably well financed. It was very active. And it was driven not by a set of negotiable political demands, but by religious fanaticism. The second was the attempt by states – some highly unstable and repressive – to develop nuclear weapons.

Blair argued that this was not the time to err on the side of caution, not a time for the worldly wise who favoured playing it long, their cynicism at best naïve and, at worst, a dereliction. And finally:

The essence of a community is common rights and responsibilities. We have obligations in relation to each other. If we are threatened we have a right to act. And we do not accept in a community that others have a right to oppress and brutalize their people. We value the freedom and dignity of the human race and each individual in it. That is the struggle which engages us. In the end believe your political leaders or not as you will. But do so at least having understood their minds.

It was a plea for his critics to look again at the evidence: the bleak intelligence reports, the consensus that weapons of mass destruction were being stockpiled and would fall into the hands of fanatics, and the subsequent threat to national security. But condemnation was unabated: from those who found Blair disingenuous, to those who believed that because his attention was elsewhere, the Government had squandered the opportunity to improve public services at home. And there were those who opposed the war from the outset, who would oppose any war in any circumstances and left Blair without a fig-leaf for cover. They denounced him a traitor and a liar who had deceived the country and Parliament, arguing that Iraq posed no direct or immediate threat to Britain, that Iraq's weapons of mass destruction, even on Britain's evidence, were not serious enough to warrant war without a specific UN resolution mandating military action, and that Saddam, in time, could have been contained. On 15 February 2003 an estimated one million people took to the streets of Britain's major cities to protest against the war. The word 'Bliar' was emblazoned on thousands of placards, 'the regular sort of guy' pilloried by his once loyal supporters.

While the marchers gathered, Blair was speaking at the Labour Party spring conference in Glasgow, a conference dominated by Iraq. Still he remained defiant:

As you watch your television pictures of the march, ponder this: if there are 500,000 on that march, that is still less than the number of people whose death Saddam has been responsible for. If there are one million, that is still less than the number of people who died in the wars he started.

Criticizing his judgement was one thing, but to attack his integrity was truly hard to take.

JB: *For a man deeply committed to his faith, he found it hurtful when people accused him of lying. You could have a row with Tony about government policy, but to accuse him of misleading the country, and having to face all those placards and angry faces, was something else. That was about scruples and morality and integrity. He understood, though, the depth of feeling in the country, was always realistic about the consequences of the war, and, let's face it, it was never going to be easy for a Labour Prime Minister.*

But yes, he was realistic. For example, he once said to me, after the bombing was over, that a few more people would have to die before Iraq could get back to some sort of normality. His words hit me hard. Was this the same Tony Blair whom I'd known for 20 years? It seemed so cold, but then I began to see why he said it because, at some point, politicians have to sit around a negotiating table and it's what brings them there. But why wait until a few more people have to die? It's the same situation in the Middle East. I have to say, though, that coolly acknowledging that more people had to die didn't seem to be very Christian except if you can show it was a just war. So was it? Getting rid of Saddam? Yes, it was just, despite its legality being called into question. And, you know, healing comes from understanding that the decision was also taken for national security reasons, at the same time ridding the world of a cruel dictator.

Shrugging off the barrage of criticism and loathing, Blair continues to say that he is ready to meet his Maker and answer for his decision to go to war. The Pope may have cautioned against intervention, urging him to do everything possible to

145

avoid war without a UN second resolution, but he believed again that 'it was the right thing to do'. Rejecting the advice of spiritual and political leaders illustrated his unshakeable belief in his own judgement, born from a moral certitude that defied the pope, archbishops and bishops, and that flowed from either courageous iron will or self-delusion.

Blair was certainly deluded into thinking that his experience in seeking peace in Northern Ireland, Kosovo, Sierra Leone and Afghanistan would hold him in good stead in Iraq. In the land of Saddam Hussein, the international community was dealing with a different beast. Iraq was on a different scale in its complexity and bigotry and international self-interest. '*Jus post bellum*' had been overlooked and it was only a question of time until anarchy would prevail following the removal of a dictator. Law and order were non-existent, and when restrictions were finally imposed, the minority Sunnis, who had ruled the majority Shias for centuries, resisted the fact that their control was being replaced by an elected government. Fraught with centuries of infighting and bitterness, the real war was yet to come.

Moreover, Blair and Bush had different agendas. Bush wanted to demonstrate American power after 9/11 while Blair believed that terrorism, coupled with the threat of weapons of mass destruction, was a major threat to the West. Nations had a moral duty to intervene in a country where genocide was commonplace and where the Hussein dynasty – with Saddam's two despot sons waiting in the wings – was likely to continue its odious ways for decades to come.

There was also a significant difference in how the American President and the British Prime Minister saw the war through their respective veils of religiosity. Blair was said to be appalled at Bush's messianic outburst in the Egyptian resort of Sharm-el-Sheikh in October 2005. Bush was meeting a Palestinian delegation during the Israeli–Palestine summit and explained to those gathered:

> I am driven with a mission from God. God would tell me, 'George, go fight these terrorists in Afghanistan.' And I did. And then God would tell me, 'George, go and end the tyranny in Iraq.' And I did. And now and again I feel God's words coming to me, 'Go get the Palestinians their state and get the Israelis their security and get peace in the Middle East.' And by God, I'm gonna do it.[13]

Blair preferred the language of the King James Bible that 'our soldiers in Iraq did not strive or die in vain'.

*   *   *

At the outset of his premiership, Blair was regarded as a lightweight politician, fixated by his standing in the opinion polls: ten years later he was accused of disregarding public opinion in his bellicose bid to do what he believed was right. Roy Jenkins, his friend and mentor, noted the change in his protégé with surprise and concern. Just months before his death, he said: 'The Prime Minister, far from lacking conviction, has almost too much, particularly when dealing with the world beyond Britain. He is a little Manichaean for my perhaps jaded taste; seeing matters in stark terms of good and evil, black and white.'[14] With the atrocities of war continuing to dominate the news, Blair began a charm offensive to win his way back into the affections of the British people. It was a sizeable task because the undoubted political achievements remained muffled; primarily, the removal of one of the most brutal dictatorships in living memory, an elected Iraqi government with Iraqi people voting in greater numbers than expected, and reports, latterly, suggesting that life in Iraq is beginning to return to some form of normality with the economy on the upturn in one or two areas of the country (although the world continues to hold its breath). According to the World Bank and International Monetary Fund estimates, per capita income has doubled and gross domestic product is almost twice that of neighbouring countries. Many Iraqis who were denied employment under Saddam Hussein's regime for reasons of ethnicity or refusing to join the Ba'ath party, now have jobs. Statistics aside, slight improvements in everyday living are reported, for example in Iraqi markets, where luxury items are on sale and people dare venture out to buy them.

The common view, that there are tiny green shoots emerging in Iraq, will nevertheless fail to halt the debate. In 2003, 69 per cent of people in Britain understood and supported Blair, but 12 months later, support had ebbed away and even pro-war activists became nervous. The press, and particularly the BBC, launched bitter attacks on the government, and Blair continued to plead his case. 'In making the judgement, would you prefer us to act, even if it turns out to be wrong? Or not to act and hope it's OK. And suppose we didn't act and the intelligence turned out to be right, how forgiving would people be?'[15]

JB: *When I look back to May 1997, I know Tony never, ever envisaged that he would be spending more time fighting terrorism in Afghanistan and Iraq than fighting poverty and other issues at home. But when bombings were carried out on British streets, then terrorism became a national issue. What was a moral cause, confronting tyranny and dictators guilty of genocide, became a question of defending Britain's streets. I know people say that the London bombings were a direct result of the invasion, but that's simply not true. Terrorist attacks were happening in cities all over the world. It didn't just start with Iraq.*

As far as the Party is concerned, Tony, to an extent, moved towards winning back the left by pushing Bush on the Israeli–Palestinian dispute, on climate change and aid to Africa. It didn't compensate for Iraq in their eyes, but at least they can say, as Dennis Skinner did, that he was on the right track with other issues.

I know there's no point in pretending that Iraq has been anything other than divisive. Of course it has. But hopefully people will look back and look at the situation now and see that slowly things are changing for the better. More than anything, Tony believed that the prospect of ridding Iraq of Saddam Hussein was a risk worth taking and that the world would be a better place without him. Yet, he also said that military action would be a waste of time if the terrible conditions were allowed to continue as before, because poverty and oppression make the work of terrorists easy and attractive, especially to young people.

Blair's conduct in Iraq has been examined in minute detail and cleared by four inquiries and a General Election. Yet possibly one of the tragedies of the war – much to the delight of odious regimes in Zimbabwe, Darfur and Burma – is that the cause of liberal interventionism has been irrevocably damaged by the Iraq invasion. Blair continues to stress that it would be catastrophic if the war ended all attempts to promote the rule of law and order around the world: that peace continues to depend on the extent to which countries are willing to work together to fight for basic freedoms.

In a speech in November 2007, Jonathan Powell, Blair's former Chief of Staff, spelled out why the West should not fear intervention.

> We can't protect our industries from competition by erecting tariff barriers and we can't protect our citizens from terrorist attack simply by better border controls. If we stand by while other peoples are brutally suppressed in other parts of the world, from Kosovo to Iraq, and if we turn a blind eye when countries disintegrate into anarchy, as we did in Afghanistan and Somalia, we will face the consequences at home.[16]

The debate about the morality of liberal interventionism will continue. The debate about military action in Iraq will concentrate the minds of historians and academics for years to come. The debate about the deployment of British troops in four wars under a Labour Prime Minister will impact on party thinking for decades. But in retrospect, the signs were there for all to see from the very outset of Blair's political life: he came to power promising an ethical dimension to foreign policy that, in time, became an ethical foreign policy. When he was appointed leader of the Party, he said he did not come into politics to change the Party but to change the country. It was an understatement. Blair came into politics to change the world, premised on fire meeting fire, and he was prepared to gamble his reputation and premiership in the process.

As a result, his popularity may have withered on the vine but the ever-optimistic former Prime Minister believes that in the intervening years, people will judge him, historians will judge him, and God, too, will be his judge – and all will do so kindly.

CHAPTER 8

Three Times a Winner

When you're abroad, you're a statesman: when you're at home you're just a politician.[1]

If the Sovereign can have an *annus horribilis*, so can her Prime Minister. Tony Blair's nadir was the year 2004. The year brought with it a string of problems that dragged him down to the point where resignation seemed the only answer.

In January, the long-awaited Hutton Inquiry report was published that lambasted the BBC but was only mildly critical of the Government; the media labelled the report a whitewash and it failed to bring the expected closure. The death toll in Iraq continued to rise with no apparent end to the insurgency and little progress in forming an elected government; for the first time since Labour came to power, the Conservatives were on level pegging; in March, sleaze allegations made by Carole Caplin's former lover, Peter Foster, made unwelcome headlines; an incident involving one of the children shocked Blair to the core, forcing him to ask whether another term in office was worth the candle; and further treatment for an irregular heart murmur was on the cards as his health continued to cause concern. Tony Blair was unwell, unloved and demotivated. The press called it Blair's Wobble, something impossible to imagine three years earlier when the darling of Labour won an historic second term at Number 10.

These were heady days. During the election campaign, New Labour had demonstrated its vision for reform and the electorate was persuaded that the Party had the experience to see it through. Blair's Cabinet colleagues also believed that the Prime Minister was a changed man – tough, sure of his own judgement, determined to refocus on domestic issues, pushing for choice and diversity in education and health, for a new breed of foundation hospitals, for greater independence for state schools – a list of policies that directly challenged old Labour's preference for equality over excellence.

At the top of Blair's agenda was education. And if liberal interventionism was the clearest example of religion shaping his foreign policy agenda, the question of education reform brought into sharp focus the influence of the Prime Minister's Christian beliefs at home. The pre-election mantra was 'education, education, education' that won him respect and votes, but where was the action to match the fine words?

Blair believed that local authorities were the main stumbling block to fundamental change in schools. Given a range of proposals for consideration, he put two at the top of his to-do list: head teachers should be helped to become more business-like in running their schools, and faith schools and city academies should be expanded to facilitate a high standard of education and morality.

It was the question of Blair's unswerving support for faith schools that raised eyebrows in Whitehall and called into question his resolve to impose a church school ethos on the education system.

In 2001, a Church of England inquiry recommended a substantial expansion of their schools, mainly in the secondary sector. In a separate report, the Department of Education produced a Green Paper that welcomed the idea of an expansion of faith-based schools in what many suspected was a co-ordinated response by the Church of England and the Government. However, after the riots in Bradford and Oldham in the summer of 2001, educationalists and sociologists again questioned the wisdom of segregating schoolchildren by religion. Others objected to public funds being used to promote religion, arguing that it went beyond the remit of education and state in an open society.

Blair and Schools Minister Stephen Timms, also a devout Christian, rejected calls to abandon the Green Paper, and the expansion of faith schools was given the go ahead. In March 2002, the Government announced that £121 million would be set aside to fund 44 new religious schools, despite growing concern among senior Whitehall figures and MPs who pleaded with Blair to, at least, amend the proposals. Frank Dobson suggested an amendment that would limit the selection rights of faith schools, requiring them to offer at least 25 per cent of places to children of another, or no, religion.

After months of squabbling, the Church of England agreed to Dobson's proposal while the Catholic Church dug in its heels, urging all 2,000 Catholic schools to lobby their MPs to scrap the plan. The Government capitulated. A feeble compromise was reached by which the Catholic Church could voluntarily offer places to non-Catholic children but the selection process would not be enforced by law. The voluntary solution was meaningless, said critics, and to enrage them still further, the Government announced that churches would no longer be required to contribute the 10 per cent of building costs that they had been paying towards construction. Opponents demanded to know why, when the taxpayer was paying the piper, the churches were calling the tune.

The warning bells grew ever louder; Britain was sleepwalking towards religious extremism by segregating Christian, Jewish and Muslim children. Doubts were raised from a wide range of people and organizations. The UN had firmly recommended mixed religious and mixed race group schools. Forty-seven per cent of head teachers in the UK believed there should be fewer, or no, faith schools. 'Handing over children to the preachers is wrong in principle and dangerous in practice' warned the *Economist*.[2] Barry Sheerman, chairman of the Commons Education Select Committee, warned that religious schools posed a threat to the cohesion of multicultural communities. 'Do you want a ghettoized education system?' he asked.

The disquiet was brushed aside. Blair had no intention of backing down, while Christian groups pitched in, offering to run city academies in deprived areas. Addressing a packed meeting of mainly evangelical Christians, organized by Faith-works in 2005, Blair singled out the group's role in education, praising their help in establishing five new academy schools. 'Here in the UK we should be proud of the work of the churches; proud of the commitment of the British people. I think that faith schools have a strong role to play.'

David Blunkett declared that he wanted to 'bottle Christian school magic for children' but membership of secular organizations mushroomed to oppose segregating children by faith. Secularists argued that the so-called special quality of faith schools was nothing to do with children but the fervour of parents. Polly Toynbee, president of the British Humanist Society, wrote: 'If prayer is what the Government demands to win a place in its most selective state schools, that's what parents must do. These schools would be near empty if they admitted only genuine believers.'[3]

Blair's strong moral stance on most aspects of government policy but particularly education, prevented him from listening to those advisers who were at variance with his Christian principles. No matter how many surveys and reports underlined the dangers of segregating children by religion, his support for church schools was unwavering: faith schools were providers of high-quality education, promoted tolerance and understanding and a sense of morality that contributed to children's achievements. Against the advice of head teachers and civil servants, he saw the expansion of church schools paving the way to an all-encompassing society where children could be taught a set of moral values that would hold them in good stead into adulthood.

So the religious fervour of the most overtly Christian prime minister for more than a century was key to the church school expansion and funding programme. Dozens of new religious schools have opened across the country with policy decisions handed to the School Organization Committees and two out of five votes given to church representatives. It was against the strongest possible advice of David Bell, Head of the Office for Standards in Education.

> I worry that many young people are being educated in faith-based schools with little appreciation of their wider responsibilities and obligations to British society. The growth in faith schools needs to be carefully but sensitively monitored by Government to ensure that pupils receive an understanding of not only their own faith but of other faiths and the wider tenets of British society.[4]

Bell criticized Islamic schools in particular, calling them a threat to national identity. But Blair's utopian aspirations were matched by his determination to push ahead with expansion, demonstrating yet again that he saw politics as the facilitator of morality.

Blair's close advisers heeded the debate and took some comfort from the fact that the Prime Minister was at last devoting more time to domestic issues. After the 2001 election, Philip Gould had warned repeatedly that if he failed to put public sector reform back on track within the first six months, the second term would be judged much as the first. A second term must make real progress and deliver on schools, hospitals and crime, policies that had faltered during New Labour's first term. In the summer of 2001, Blair holidayed in Mexico, and spent much of the time working on plans to tie domestic reform to an increase in spending. By September, education, health and crime issues were top of the agenda and Blair seemed to relish the challenge. But the resolve was short lived. On 11 September, everything changed. Blair, who was attending the TUC Conference in Brighton when terrorists attacked the United States, was whisked back to London amid tight security. Domestic policy issues were pushed to one side as the Prime Minister was thrust back on the world stage. Afghanistan, Al Qaeda, the Taliban, Osama bin Laden – these were the names on his lips while diversity and choice in the public sector were, if not forgotten, then relegated for the foreseeable future.

Blair spent the following year flying 40,000 miles and attended 54 meetings with world leaders, acting as broker in an attempt to secure international support for dealing with the Taliban. It was a mammoth and stressful task that consumed his time and energy. One close aide said it was almost impossible to find a slot in his diary for domestic issues, and despite the need to focus on the home front, Blair was blown off course by the dramatic events in New York and Washington. The task fell to Gordon Brown who believed that domestic policy was, in any event, in the gift of the Treasury. It was an expediency that Blair would live to regret; the Prime Minister and the Chancellor had very different agendas.

Brown believed there was no reason to place choice and diversity in the public sector at the top of the Government's reform agenda; the question of establishing foundation hospitals saw bullets fly between the Blair and Brown camps; the Chancellor remained firmly opposed to the Euro (virtually kicking it out of touch in June 2003), and as tension mounted over the prospect of war, Brown distanced himself from the Prime Minister, keeping his head well below the parapet, a deafening silence in the growing clamour to oppose the invasion.

In the following months, Blair's frequent absence from the UK and Brown's hands-on Chancellorship gave rise to the Treasury view that Blair had become Britain's non-executive chairman while Brown was chief executive. It was a particularly dark period in the relationship between the two men when Blair finally conceded that the real opposition to government was no longer the Tory Party but the Chancellor.

JB: *It should have been a time of rejoicing and consolidation. Winning a second term had been an obsession with the Party because we had never won two full terms before and this was the dream, establishing the Party as the natural party of government. Tony was determined to use the second term to take us further down the road of reform but there was always this constant battle with Gordon who held the purse strings, like a kid going to his parents for pocket money. The rivalry was completely out of hand. Then of course Iraq took up so much of his time. Tony couldn't do it all, it goes without saying. But who could have predicted 9/11? Sometimes I try to think what might have been if 9/11 and Iraq hadn't happened, if Tony had been able to give more time to issues that people really cared about, that affected their lives; but it doesn't do any good thinking like that, does it?*

It was one of the most difficult times I can remember. We'd

always managed to have a pint together and a laugh or two, remi-
niscing about old times, but it wasn't the time for banter. We had
to sit back and see how it would all unfold and how he would
come out at the other end, and he did.

There was little to smile about in the months ahead. The relationship with Brown deteriorated further as Blair tried to inch
back onto home territory, determined, despite Iraq, to focus
on home affairs, although to a large extent Brown hemmed
him in. The Chancellor continued to oppose Blair's plans to
increase choice and diversity, and positively raged when Blair
rekindled an interest in pensions. To add to Blair's woes, the
fire brigade union began a series of 48-hour strikes. Could it
get any worse?

It could, and did, with a vengeance. Cherie's friendship
with Carole Caplin, a lifestyle guru who advised Cherie on
everything from clothes to health, was about to erupt. Cherie
decided to buy two apartments in Bristol, one for son Euan
while he was at university and another as an investment.
Unbeknown to Blair, negotiations for the purchase of the
flats were in the hands of Peter Foster, a convicted conman
who was also Caplin's lover. The *Mail on Sunday* was first with
the story that torpedoed the Blairs for weeks. It was a miser-
able time for the family, and Blair's anger turned on the
media as he looked on sympathetically at the savage treatment of his wife. The episode came to an end, temporarily,
when Cherie made an emotional speech at Millbank and,
close to tears, reminded us, 'I am not superwoman.' In her
autobiography, Cherie recalled the ordeal: 'Never before, or

since, have I felt myself hounded. I was their [photographers'] prey. It was that simple. The worst aspect of the affair was that I had let Tony down. At the moment in his life when he most needed me, I was a drag on his energies rather than a source of support.'[5]

JB: *The Caplin saga was one of the most bizarre of Tony's time at Number 10. It was one of those situations that just got out of hand. Certainly Cherie, in the early days, had little interest in fashion and make-up and the like, and she needed help. The newspapers were always having a go at her for her lack of dress sense and style. Then, when she decided to do something about it and took Carole on to help, they hammered even harder. There's no doubt Cherie smartened up and started to look good, but why she allowed Carole to take over her life, I'll never know. It caused ructions with Alastair who kept reminding them she was trouble, not to mention others at Downing Street like Fiona and Anji Hunter who kept saying she should be kept at arms' length. But Cherie refused to ditch her. Eventually she had to get rid of her, but not until there'd been a great deal of heartache. And for what? She could have had advice from anyone she liked. It's not as though Carole could tell them anything new as a lifestyle guru. Cut down on fats and salt. Eat more fruit and veg, that sort of thing. I remember Tony coming here to 'Myrobella' and asking for an elderflower tea. I said 'Bugger off and have coffee like the rest of us.' He took the hint.*

The press called it Cheriegate, and the long-drawn-out episode placed tremendous strain on the family, coming at a time of international tension and internal party squabbling, at the heart of which was the question of when Blair would stand down. Brown was obsessed with the idea of the top job, and with little agreement on key issues, and a government already two years into its second term, the Party was beginning to look frail and confused. Deputy Prime Minister John Prescott intervened, forcefully telling them at a secret meeting at Admiralty House: 'If you carry on as you are, you will destroy the Labour Party. And I won't let you do that.' Not that the warning had any significant, long-term effect. Cherie put it in graphic terms: 'Gordon continued to rattle the keys over Tony's head and Tony suffered a crisis of confidence as to whether he was still an asset to the Labour Party.'[6]

Despite the economy performing well, Blair's personal rating had fallen dramatically, with thousands of people reeling at the horrific, nightly television pictures from Iraq. The once-cheery 'Tone' was tumbling into depression; he looked gaunt and tired as the emerging chaos in Iraq, and allegations that he had tricked Britain into going to war, dominated the headlines. It was the worst possible time for the series of disasters that was to follow. The Hutton Inquiry report had been expected at the end of 2003 and the long wait was uncomfortable. Hutton finally reported on 17 January, and while criticizing the BBC, Lord Hutton was seen to have let the Government off lightly. The press unanimously agreed that the report was a whitewash and, worse, avoided the fundamental question of whether Blair had taken Britain to war under false pretences. On 4 February, Blair was forced to announce a further inquiry under Lord Butler whose remit was to investigate the nature of British intelligence.

Then, when the family had reason to believe Cheriegate was behind them, Peter Foster, Carole Caplin's rogue lover, came back to haunt them. In an interview in an Australian newspaper, Foster made lurid allegations about the relationship between Caplin and the Blairs. Equally disturbing for Blair the family man was the effect the publicity was having on his older children, such was the animosity directed at their once popular father. In March 2004, a particular incident involving one of the children stunned him and left him wondering whether the family could take any more. (The Press Complaints Council intervened on behalf of the Blairs and the press agreed not to reveal details of the incident.) The Brown camp seized the moment of the family's despair to offer to find an honourable exit for Blair; a domestic crisis might be an excellent way for the Prime Minister to depart Number 10 and one that would also win public sympathy.

Anthony Seldon observed: 'Scenting blood, the Brownites kept up the pressure which they hoped would destroy him. It was the endless, psychological drain of the warfare with Gordon that got him down. It went on and on and it sucked his energy dry' quotes an aide.[7]

So how close did Blair come to handing the keys of Number 10 to the Chancellor? He was on the very edge. Resignation seemed the only answer, although close colleagues, and Cherie, thought otherwise.

JB: *Yes, it was a sticky patch, and although all government is difficult, this was something else again. Tony was exhausted and depressed and it took him some time to recover, but if you think of what was happening at the time, it wasn't surprising. The press were giving him a hard time so the PR people swung into even greater action and it was a double-edged sword really because Labour couldn't get away from the spin label, no matter what they did. It changed the whole view of government. It changed me to an extent because when people were talking to me about Tony or government policy, I would be thinking, 'Why are they telling me this?' and alarm bells would start ringing. Yet he always said that there is no point being in politics unless you strive for what you believe in, freedom, democratic values, but his values had to be tempered by the real world of politics. I know he hadn't been well and there was a lot of pressure with the Hutton Inquiry and the news coming out of Iraq, but I would have been amazed if he'd stood down then. Certainly Cherie was against him going, as were a majority of the Cabinet. If he had the health and strength – although his health wasn't good for a while – then he always said it was a privilege to do the job, that's what he wanted; but at the end of the day, his life wouldn't end when the job ended. Tony always knew that there was a lot more he wanted to do when he finally left office.*

But the pressure was enormous. There was a limit to what he could do overseas and he never seemed to go for the easy option. People always said, 'What business is it of ours if people in Sierra Leone or Kosovo are dying?' Well it was, and is our business when it's militarily possible to stop the killings. Isn't it all rooted in the Christian faith? I find it very difficult to understand how members of the Labour Party can think otherwise.

Blair had said throughout his premiership that if he became a liability to the Party and the country, he would resign. After seven years as Prime Minister, he came to the conclusion that the Party and the country would be better off without him. It was time to go. Moreover, the opinion polls, prior to the May local elections, indicated a 'white-out' for the Government, a bleak outlook for New Labour. In the event, Labour lost over 450 seats: a poor result, but not nearly as bad as predicted. The result made Blair think again, and close colleagues, chivvied by Cherie, rallied round, cajoling and coaxing, appealing to his ego, telling him that he was the only person to lead Labour to a third victory. Was it possible? Blair's confidence slowly returned, much to the dismay of the Chancellor who reportedly flounced into his office shouting, 'When the fuck are you going to fuck off and give me a date? I want the job now.'[8] Brown's gentle plea fell on deaf ears. If there was a chance of carrying on, Blair would take it, mainly because his legacy was still mired in Iraq, there was little progress on public sector reform, and power sharing negotiations in Northern Ireland remained unresolved.

By June, the wobble had steadied. Blair was ready to stand up to his critics and a sullen Chancellor. There were one or two encouraging signs: Lord Butler reported that the Prime Minister had not lied over taking the country to war, the UN Security Council passed a resolution endorsing the appointment of an interim government in Iraq, and improvements were being seen in hospitals and schools after the Government's large injection of funds. In the autumn, with one eye on a 2005 General Election, he announced a five-year plan to push through public service reforms. Tony Blair was back on course, stamping his authority on health, education and law and order.

At the Labour Party Conference, he set out ten pointers to a third term Labour Government and what it would mean for families – more choice for mums, more jobs in every region of the UK, more choice in education, wider opportunities to obtain mortgages – little was left out. But would he, as the press predicted, brush aside Iraq? He dealt with it head-on.

> The evidence about Saddam having actual biological and chemical weapons, as opposed to the capability to develop them, has turned out to be wrong. I simply point out that such evidence was agreed by the whole international community, not least because Saddam had used such weapons against his own people and neighbouring countries. And the problem is, I can apologize for the information that turned out to be wrong but I can't sincerely at least for removing Saddam. The world is a better place with Saddam in prison and not in power.[9]

This was as near an apology that Blair was ever going to make. It was also a frail attempt at healing the wounds of some conference delegates who continued to heckle, 'You've got blood on your hands.'

The Conference speech made plain that Blair was back in charge and setting the agenda. So why did he make the extraordinary decision to pre-announce his departure the day after Conference, admitting that he would fight a third election but not a fourth? Close colleagues were astounded. 'It was a very foolish, indeed mad thing to do', said the ultra Blairite Alan Milburn.[10] Blair shrugged off the criticism and started planning his final months in power.

JB: *Tony's the first to admit now that it wasn't the best move in the world, saying he would step down after a third term. It didn't take much working out that he would never be able to serve a full term, that at some point he would have to hand over to his successor before the end of the third term to give a new leader the chance to establish himself. What were his so-called advisers doing? Why didn't they challenge him? I know that he wanted to set out his plans for the future, but this was one step too far and he knows it. Trouble is, those around him were telling him what they thought he wanted to hear, pussy-footing and saying that he had made up his mind, so there was no point in challenging him. But he was down at the time and his confidence had been knocked. It needed someone to tell him that while he might well decide to step down before a fourth term, it was unwise to say so from Day One. People would always be asking 'Hey, what's going on here? When are you going?' And of course that's just what happened.*

Brown was on a visit to Washington when he heard of the Prime Minister's future plans. He was furious, accusing Blair of deliberately waiting until he was out of the country before announcing his decision to fight a third election. There is no evidence to suggest that the announcement was timed to coincide with Brown's absence, but as one aide said, 'It was certainly one in the eye and a bloody convenient time from our point of view.' On this occasion, the Chancellor was forced to contain his anger. The following morning Blair had heart surgery to correct an irregular heartbeat. Brown, through gritted teeth, sent him best wishes for a speedy recovery, knowing that revenge would be his at a more appropriate time.

The operation was a success. Only days later, Blair said he felt ready to get on with the job, and as 2005 approached he had reason to feel mildly optimistic. There was encouraging news from Northern Ireland, the Iraqi election in January 2005 was well supported despite terrorist threats, and on the home front the Government was pushing ahead with foundation hospitals and university top-up fees. Modest improvements were becoming apparent, and although political commentators continued their gloomy forecasts that Blair was heading for defeat, opinion polls showed Labour well ahead of the Opposition.

Despite Labour's lead, the 2005 election proved to be the most difficult of Blair's three campaigns. 'Britain Forward, Not Back' was the most detailed of the three Manifestos, yet lack of trust dogged the campaign; not only the electorate but the Party were asking, 'Can we trust the Blair Government again?' Efforts to focus on domestic issues were overshadowed by the Iraq invasion. Day after day, the Prime Minister was branded a liar over the decision to go to war. Day after day, he feared the outcome of the election, and the polls confirmed he was right to be nervous; Labour's lead had fallen to just 2 per cent. Smarting from Blair's decision to continue for another term, Brown sulked in his Treasury sanctuary, and when Alan Milburn was asked to mastermind the election campaign, his mood plummeted into darkness. The theory was that Blair planned to run the campaign without his Chancellor and, true or not, the story made front-page headlines. Finally Brown took heed of his aides who advised him that continued bickering would not only cause immense damage to the Party but would sabotage his chances of becoming Prime Minister in a third term. Brown dispensed with the vitriol and became honey-tongued, recanting and enjoying the moment of the knight in shining armour galloping to Blair's rescue. Philip Gould believed it was the turning point in the election campaign. Others sighed wearily, convinced that Blair's reliance on Brown's support weakened his position still further.

JB: *Everyone was being so negative – the press, the pollsters, the politicians. Tony rang me mid-way through the campaign and asked how it was going. I said I thought it was going all right. And he said quietly, 'Not you too. What do you mean, only all right?' It was getting to him. When he finally arrived in the constituency, he was convinced we would lose the election. Everyone was sitting around 'Myrobella' looking glum and twitchy, and Tony kept asking for the latest updates from Party headquarters. When the results came in and we heard Labour had lost Putney, it really got to him and he just disappeared into another room by himself. I'm sure he said a prayer or two . . . then he wandered out into the garden. It was freezing, but he had to get out. At best he thought we might end up with a majority of around 40 and that would have made life very difficult. At the end of the day though, our* *prayers were answered. We ended up with a majority of 66; not perfect, but in those post-Iraq days it was a respectable working majority.*

Blair's place in the history books was secured by the simple statistical fact of winning three elections, but he wanted his legacy to be more than a mere statistic. He had been Prime Minister for eight years, the maximum period allowed by American presidents and longer than most British prime ministers. His critics believed that although progress was made in the second term, in health, education, welfare and crime prevention, opportunities for change had been wasted and policies had been insufficiently radical primarily because the term was dominated by Iraq. A third term would define his premiership, and the world would see Blair's domestic and foreign policies mature and prosper. It was a considerable undertaking, made more difficult still by the pre-announcement of his departure.

The scale of the task was epitomized in a rollercoaster 24-hour period two months after the election. Blair was beginning to think that his fortunes had turned around when, after two days lobbying in Singapore – with Paris the clear favourite – Britain won the bid to host the Olympics in 2012. It was commonly believed that Blair's last-minute intervention swung the delegates in favour of the UK. Before the decision was announced, he flew back to Scotland for the G8 conference. Months of detailed work had gone into preparing for the Conference and again it looked as though Blair's efforts might have paid off. On arrival, he was told that Bush was listening more attentively to warnings on climate change: Blair had lobbied him at a meeting in Washington the previous month. At that same meeting, Blair pleaded for the G8 to boost aid to Africa by $50 billion; he was told the Americans had agreed to double aid to Africa. Blair had cause to raise a smile. The G8 was already well on its way to being the most successful conference to date, and Olympics 2012 was heading to London. How the troubled days of April and May seemed a long way off.

But if a week is a long time in politics, Tony Blair saw the world turning on its head in just 12 hours. On Thursday, 7 July, terrorists came to London. Three Islamic suicide bombers blew themselves up at different stations on the London Underground and a fourth detonated a bomb on a Number 30 bus. Fifty-six innocent people lost their lives and 700 people were injured, many seriously. It was the deadliest bombing in London since the Second World War.

JB: *It hit him hard. He'd been warned of possible threats on many occasions. When John Stevens was in charge of the Metropolitan Police, Tony was told that 12 attacks had been foiled over a five-year period, so he knew it was coming at some point, but the worst thing for Tony was that the suicide bombers were all British. The tragedy completely took the shine off the Olympics announcement. Who wanted to celebrate after what had happened? Who could believe that in 24 hours, we could win the Olympics bid, move forward on aid to Africa and climate change, and then have to deal with the London bombings? Some people of course blamed Tony for the bombings, that we had put Britain in the firing line because of Iraq and Afghanistan. But it was ridiculous to think that somehow we could avoid the threat of terrorism by refusing to stand up to rogue states. We were already a target because of the action in Afghanistan, and what message would it give out to terrorists that if we agreed to play by their rules, we'd be safe? You can't do business like that. And who believed anyway that Tony's work in Kosovo, rescuing the Muslim community there, or his work in the Middle East, would make any positive difference to the suicide bombers? Of course not. We were on their target list whatever happened in Iraq.*

As frequently happens in times of national crises, the Prime Minister's handling of the situation boosted his authority within the Party and the country. Moreover, progress on public sector reform was working in the Government's favour and memos were fired off reminding the Party that the next six months would be crucial. For a short period, Blair allowed himself to believe that any immediate challenge to his leadership was on the wane, at a time when he was more certain than ever about the future direction of government and what he wanted to achieve. Forging ahead on choice within the NHS, education reform (on target with the Education and Inspections Bill), more faith schools and city academies, there was progress, too, on energy, climate change and pensions. The strategy and investment were starting to come good and it was by far one of the most fruitful times of his premiership. Philip Gould saw his boss concentrating on issues that he had urged upon him five years earlier:

It has been in Blair's third term that most progress has been made towards turning that vision into serious policy reality, with choice becoming a given in the NHS and our education system now genuinely moving towards diversity. It is clear that modernization has filled out as a concept over the years of government, gradually emerging as a big idea based on giving power to individuals in a world of change.[11]

The upswing could not last. In November, Blair suffered his first defeat as Prime Minister over the Terrorist Bill, which was a major blow to his authority. And there was an unexpected black cloud hovering overhead. Blair's reputation was damaged still further when the 'cash for honours' affair reared its ugly head. In March 2006, the Metropolitan Police launched an investigation into whether Labour was guilty of offering peerages in return for donations, an investigation that dogged him until after he left office.

The question of when Blair would stand down was posed almost daily in newspapers and on television. His team of advisers also began to press for a date to end the speculation. Somehow he seemed reluctant to answer the question. Had he not won a third election victory? Had he not shown Labour to be the natural party of government? Why should he not continue until at least 2008? Such was the rhetoric until events in early September 2006, just before the start of the Labour Party Conference, brought matters to a head.

On the morning of 6 September 2006, the headlines made

grim reading for the Prime Minister. He was staring down the barrel of a shotgun, and the finger on the trigger was that of his old friend, the Chancellor.

Resignation and Threats:
The Plot to Oust the Prime Minister

It's Time to Pack your Bags and Go, Tony

The Day Blair Accused his Chancellor of Blackmail

Ten years of brooding had finally boiled over. The message from Brown to Blair was ugly and unequivocal: 'Do as I say or you'll be bundled from office.' In a sign of the fierce power struggle raging at the top, Brown demanded a timetable for the Prime Minister's departure, that the timetable be made public and, regardless of the constitutional implications, ordered Blair to put in place a joint premiership. Unwilling to give up the fight without a struggle, Blair used the full power of office to hold out. Whatever innocent interpretation was given in press briefings, he recognized an attempted coup when it stared him in the face. One insider remarked: 'Threatening a Prime Minister in this way borders on the unconstitutional. We are a democracy, not an autocracy living in the era of the Soviet Union circa 1956. There is no way people can be muzzled in the way the Chancellor is demanding.'

It was a clumsy attempt to remove a Prime Minister who, 15 months earlier, had won a third election victory and a mandate to govern. Angry at the unsavoury machinations of the Party he had kept in power for a decade, Blair was forced to announce his resignation, although he was determined to go at a time of his choosing. The next day, he told the world's press that he would stand down within a year and would attend his final Labour Party Conference as leader. The following weekend, the *Observer* revealed that up to ten Cabinet Ministers were discussing an 'anyone but Gordon' candidate, threatening to make the contest an attack on Brown's integrity.

JB: *After all the threats and the shouting matches, the plotters got cold feet. Gordon Brown got cold feet. His team had chipped and chipped away over the years, but nothing matched their ridiculous behaviour this time round, trying to oust a constitutionally elected prime minister. If it had happened in a third-world country, politicians worldwide would have condemned it. What was the point? Tony had no intention of staying on indefinitely, so all the infighting was for nothing. Think about it. It was no coincidence that the ultimatum came just before the Party Conference because they wanted a public hanging, to knock him off at the conference. What sort of message would that have been to the country?*

What many MPs conveniently forgot was that they were there because of Tony. Some had won seats that would never have fallen to Labour but for the Blair effect, and it goes without saying that a number of them will lose those seats at the next election.

I still remember Tony's speech at Quinton Kynaston School, the day he announced that he would stand down in a year. 'First thing to do is apologize on behalf of the Labour Party for the last week which, with everything going on back here and in the world, has not been our greatest hour.' How right he was.

The question asked time and again is why Tony refused to move Gordon when he was so openly hostile. We all remember the headline, 'Brown is now the official opposition to Blairite Labour'. Some say Tony was too weak. Others say it was out of loyalty. Yet not only did he put up with him, he tried to protect him.

The press had a field day and posed two questions – how much longer could Blair hold on, and was Brown fit to be Prime Minister? Brown tried to defuse the situation by repeatedly denying he had any knowledge of the coup, but there were few who believed his protests. The damage to the Government was considerable. Blair could look to another nine months in office, and a frantic period of activity in which to finish the job.

A period of calm descended on the Party. Brown was keen to be seen as conciliatory, particularly over public service reform that had been one of the triggers for hostilities between the Blair and Brown camps. In March 2007, to the astonishment of Downing Street, Brown gave his full support to Blair's Policy Review that consisted of six working groups looking at personalized public services. The Chancellor even backed the controversial city academies programme. 'Whisper it softly, but Brownites and Blairites are starting to work together' said Peter Riddell in *The Times*. 'On policy Mr Brown is determined to ensure that New Labour carries on post-Blair.'[12]

It was stretching credibility to believe that Brown had seen the error of his ways; more likely, he agreed with his advisers who told him it was unwise to be seen as anti-reform. Relations between the two sides were cordial, even warm. But, sayeth the soothsayer, 'Let those who desire peace, prepare for war.' The day after the launch of the Policy Review – Black Tuesday – the former head of the Civil Service, Lord Turnbull, threw the book at Brown, accusing him of Stalinist ruthlessness. With Tory chants in the Commons that this was the Chancellor's week from hell, Lord Turnbull alleged that Brown belittled Ministers, treated colleagues with contempt, shirked unpopular decisions, and disappeared at difficult moments for the Government. For good measure, he added: 'He has a Macavity quality. He's not there when there is dirty work to be done.'[13]

The bloggers had a field day:

Macavity, Macavity, there's no one like Macavity,
there never was a cat of such deceitfulness and suavity.
He always had an alibi and one or two to spare,
and whatever time the leak took place,
Macavity wasn't there.

It was an astonishing attack at every level, and it was the unlikely figure of Tony Blair who came to Brown's rescue. Blair claimed that Lord Turnbull's outburst was unacceptable from someone who had once criticized civil servants for attacking political masters in their memoirs. But disagreeable questions continued to be asked of the under-siege Chancellor. Would he change if he got the top job? Should he be allowed to remain unopposed? *The Times* mischievously published photographs of other 'unopposed' leaders, including King Jong II of North Korea, President Suharto of Indonesia, Aleksandr Lukashenko of Belarus and Saddam Hussein.

It was a bizarre period in British politics. And what does it tell us about Blair, the friend and colleague? Was it a case of turning the other cheek? Or did he believe that the future of the Party, and his legacy, relied on a smooth transition to a Brown premiership?

JB: *We all knew that their relationship was like a stormy marriage – all the passion, the anger, the jealousy and who promised what to the other? How many times it looked as though they were heading for the divorce courts? But as I saw it, there had always been this mix of respect and frustration, high regard and mistrust. In the early days, Tony certainly believed that Gordon should take over when the time was right. He used to say, why shouldn't he be ambitious? But at no point did he name Gordon as his successor – it wasn't in his gift – although he supported him whenever he could, even during the early months of 2007 after Gordon tried to derail him.*

It was interesting on two counts. To offer support to someone who had behaved so badly was the loyal Tony Blair that I knew so well. Most people would have been out for revenge. But was he doing it for the sake of his legacy? I don't think so, because by then, he'd just about done all he could and was winding down. I think it was more complicated. It was always a love–hate relationship. Gordon had been very good to him in the early days and they'd worked closely on reforming the Party. Together with Peter

Mandelson, they had created New Labour. There was a mutual respect, and Tony always said he was a good Chancellor. If only Gordon had been more supportive, or at least less obstructive, it could have been one of the great political partnerships of all time. I think it also showed as far as Cherie was concerned that, despite rumours to the contrary, Tony was his own man. There's no way Cherie would have dug Gordon out of a hole after Lord Turnbull's outburst. She never wanted him to have the job. But Tony stuck to his guns, and with all Gordon's problems since becoming Prime Minister, Tony has been careful not to criticize.

In his final six months at Number 10, political journalists and commentators analysed Blair's premiership in minute detail; the consensus seemed to be that Tony Blair had been the most skilled and gifted politician of his generation. However, there was little consensus beyond his general aptitude for the job. As he gave notice that he was finally bowing out, many, in and out of the Labour Party, believed he had wasted the opportunities of the Blair years, that public service reform was too little too late, and he had lost his way in a deeply unpopular war that would forever be his epitaph.

Moreover, the Catholic gay adoption row in the early months of 2007 reminded voters again that Blair's religion was always in danger of intruding on government policy. Catholic adoption agencies demanded the right to decline applications for adoption from homosexual couples, a position that would be nullified under the new Equalities Act. What started out as an ethical debate exploded into a full-blown row between Church and State. Blair struggled to find a compromise, causing Harriet Harman famously to quip, 'You can't be a little bit against discrimination.' But following five days of discussions with interested parties, Blair announced that there would be no exemption for Catholic adoption agencies and no compromise. 'People assume because he has a personal faith that the moment a bishop says "Boo" he jumps. But that's not true or he wouldn't have introduced civil partnerships or repealed Section 28. He comes from a liberal Christian tradition', said a close Cabinet colleague.[14]

To the bitter end, Blair never stopped trying to change public opinion. The 'cash for honours' investigation, that many believed was a deliberate attempt to tear apart his moral authority, overshadowed his final days, but there were still battles to be won, mainly at the EU Council in Brussels and the G8 at Heiligendamm. Despite the long arm of the law investigating cash for honours inside Number 10, he pressed on with the Policy Review reports, worked with Bush on finding an agreement on climate change, announced in the Commons that British troops in Basra would be reduced from 7,500 to 5,500, and sensing that a settlement might be possible, pushed ahead on power sharing in Northern Ireland. This was Blair's final triumph, made all the sweeter when the historic agreement was signed at Stormont, just weeks before his premiership ended. Journalists said he looked every bit the proud parent at school prize-giving.

With Northern Ireland's future secured, Blair took off on a worldwide farewell tour to Iraq, Libya, Sierra Leone and South Africa, described by some as a 'legacy tour'; others preferred to call it 'a vanity trip'. His final EU trip, as Prime

Minister, was to the G8 Conference in Heiligendamm where he championed climate change and aid to Africa.

According to Anthony Seldon, the G8 meeting achieved Blair's main objective:

> In championing climate change and Africa in his final two years, Blair had managed to re-engage with the idealism of the British public which he thought had been cemented with the idealism of his liberal interventionism but which had been damaged so badly over Iraq. He had again found how to touch the popular nerve. Over Iraq, he had been made to feel like a pariah: on these issues, even if he had not gone far enough for many, he had reconnected morally with many. And that mattered deeply to him.[15]

When the EU Council meeting finally ended in the early hours of the morning, and his political entourage had taken to their beds, Blair slipped out and took an early flight to Rome for an audience with Pope Benedict XVI. It was a more comfortable encounter than the meeting with Pope John Paul that had taken place just weeks before the Iraq war. Not surprisingly, the visit re-ignited speculation that Blair was about to be received into the Catholic Church, sparking a hostile response from those who pointed to Blair's parliamentary voting record as evidence that he was an unfit candidate for Rome.

The papal audience was a whirlwind end to a whirlwind premiership. On 17 June, Blair took Prime Minister's Questions for the final time. Cameron lavished praise on the outgoing Prime Minister who walked out of the Chamber to a standing ovation from all sides of the House.

There was still the question of his resignation speech. His advisers believed that the perfect venue would be outside Number 10. Blair thought otherwise. With Cherie and daughter Kathryn, he returned to Sedgefield where his political journey had begun 24 years earlier. It was a highly charged speech in which he apologized for his mistakes, admitted that his legacy in the eyes of many would be dominated by Iraq and pleaded with people to believe he had acted in good faith.

> Hand on heart, I did what I thought was right. I may have been wrong. That's your call. But believe one thing, if nothing else. I did what I thought was right for our country.[16]

JB: *I was told two weeks before the resignation to book Trimdon Labour Club, so I knew he would be making the speech there. I'd booked the main concert room but I'd also booked a funeral party in the bar. It was Maisie Tone's funeral that day, a real character in the village. When we agreed a few years earlier to allow women on the committee, Maisie was the first to come forward, she was one of us really, so I knew we had to have a 'do' for her. As I told Sky News, the family was amazed that so many people turned out for the funeral party. But that's village life isn't it, when you have the Prime Minister in one room on the point of resigning, and a funeral party for the family of a great old lady in the other.*

The speech . . . well it was very emotional. There were quite a few of us holding back the tears, including Tony. I suppose you could say he was wistful, could have done better, he said, pitching it at the right level – not the great 'I am'. The message I took from the speech was about not being afraid to try the impossible. Looking back, he didn't resent what happened despite the shenanigans. What he did say to me later was that he knew for sure he would have been able to deal with Cameron at the next election but he didn't believe Gordon would have it in him . . . time will tell.

It was a strange day certainly. As I said in the club . . . I started out that morning as agent to the Prime Minister, then I was agent to the MP for Sedgefield, then of course he announced he was standing down altogether, so by the evening I was out of a job.

There was something quite surreal about the whole thing. After the speech we went back to 'Myrobella' and Cherie was putting green stickers on pieces of furniture that she wanted to take back to London. Of course she didn't tell me, so I was wandering around taking them off as fast as she was putting them on. I thought it was the removal people doing it, not Cherie. It was a bit like a Brian Rix farce – the stickers, not the politics.

Expressions of undying love from his followers might have been expected, but a most unlikely bunch of admirers, political columnists and former senior Tories, were also beating their breasts at Blair's departure.

'You wait – you'll be sorry when they're gone . . .' Alice Miles, *Times* columnist:
'. . . to survive ten years in No. 10 is an extraordinarily difficult feat, particularly under the constant media scrutiny that prime ministers today have to face. To do so while raising a young family is almost superhuman . . .'[17]

'Despite himself, Blair has made Britain a better place.' Michael Portillo, former senior Tory. 'Blair will retire unlamented, after all. But he leaves behind a country more easygoing than the one he inherited, less insular and more self-confident.'[18]

'We're great again. Thanks, Tony . . .' Tim Hames, columnist who went on to claim 'that the real foreign policy legacy of the Blair years is that Britain has become the second most powerful country in the world'.[19]

And perhaps most surprising of all:

'I'm no fan of the man but I do love Blair's Britain.' Matthew Parris, former adviser to Margaret Thatcher and columnist. 'You can grab an era by the lapels as she (Thatcher) did, or you can let an era grab you by the lapels and guide it as he has; both are creative forces in politics.'[20]

Where were voices of support during the dark months, Blair might have asked? But his premiership, which ended on a surprisingly high note, was over. It was time to think about a new life outside mainstream politics.

Unusual in British political life, Tony Blair was allowed to leave office in the manner of his choosing, refusing to be bundled out like so many of his predecessors. Choosing the time of his departure gave him the unique opportunity to plan for the future, and although he insisted he had no specific plans, it was announced the following day that the former British Prime Minister had accepted the unpaid job of envoy to the Middle East for the Quartet (US, EU, UN, Russia).

Was Blair being selfless and noble in taking on the Middle East mission? Was he being egoistical or heroic? The hero is always open to the charge of self-aggrandisement, yet if ego was central to his endeavours, the actor-politician striding the world stage craving attention would indeed be making a hollow gesture. But in the cynical world of politics, it was just possible that Blair genuinely wanted to 'do the right thing', and when the opportunity was offered, it found a response and a readiness in him to go beyond mere shuffling diplomacy.

Middle East envoy was the first of several 'job' announcements, some paid, some unpaid, that would give Blair the opportunity to carve out a new life without the constraints and pressures of party, parliament and politics. He was 54 years old and believed he had much more to offer. It was time to move on, time to get to grips with a range of new experiences away from the Downing Street circus with a list of practical matters to address. He would have to learn to exist without the support of the government machine; he would learn to send text messages to his children without incurring the wrath of the security services; he could rejoice in the freedom of no longer fearing the next crisis that loomed around the corner; and, at last, he could ditch Alastair Campbell's well-meaning diktat that 'we don't do God'.

PART 3

CHAPTER 9

Post Premiership

So hope for a great sea change on the far side of revenge
Believe that a future shore is reachable from here
Believe in miracles and cures and healing wells.[1]

Tony Blair was a remarkable if controversial Prime Minister, the man who brought peace to Northern Ireland, constitutional change to mainland Britain, engaged in four wars, and belatedly, made respectable headway in improving public services. But who was he? What did we learn about Blair during his ten-year premiership? Despite his claim to be 'a regular sort of guy', his Downing Street years unmasked a man of contradiction: a high moral tone vied with hard-headed politics that helped him hang on to power; tenacity and conviction on foreign policy issues contrasted sharply with a hesitancy on the domestic front; either ultra loyal or ruthless to parliamentary colleagues; religious fervour sat alongside a penchant for show-biz; unashamedly courting public opinion yet able to ride a fierce hate campaign after the Iraq invasion; a devoted family man and a workaholic.

189

Twenty-four years as Member of Parliament for Sedgefield, of which ten were spent in the top job, Blair always knew that his political life would continue beyond his premiership, despite the relentless pressure of Number 10. But why? What drove the former Prime Minister who, after ten gruelling years, might have yearned for a quieter life, slipping serenely into semi-retirement? Why not espouse the press image that sneered at Blair the buck-grabbing celebrity, sallying forth on lecture tours, negotiating multi-million-pound book deals and bringing home even more bacon on the back of lucrative city jobs? Why suffer the possible indignity of failure in the Middle East, an indifferent response to the Inter-Faith Foundation and the myriad other causes that he promised to support? Was the former Prime Minister seeking penance as well as peace?

JB: *I remember saying to him that he could always hole up at 'Myrobella' to write the book – that's what I thought he'd be doing after he stood down. He looked at me as though I'd slapped his face. Writing books wasn't what he had in mind. Tony was only 54 when he resigned and knew he had a lot more to give on the political front. We wanted him to stay on as MP, but when the Middle East job came along, we knew we'd lost him. Other than that, he had little idea about what else he was going to do except he also had to make a living because he still had a young family to support. Obviously, he needed to balance his time between the Quartet and the two Foundations, and paid employment. And that's what he's done.*

There were certainly a number of people who, because of Iraq, had doubts about Tony's suitability for the Middle East job, but when it comes down to it he seems to have a talent for persuading unreasonable people to do reasonable things. Mainly this was seen in his work in Northern Ireland: bringing together Ian Paisley and Martin McGuinness was no mean feat. At first, everyone in Northern Ireland said the situation was hopeless because the other side didn't want peace and each side said it about the other. But when things got difficult, Tony would just sit it out, drip-feeding information that led both sides to believe that they were the ones being difficult and, when they might be blamed for holding back the political process, they would hopefully back down. The same might be true in the Middle East. The Palestinians still talk about the injustice of occupation and the Israelis express fears about their security. These are real fears that have to be dealt with as part of the bigger problem.

Blair clinched the unpaid job of international envoy to the Middle East courtesy of the Quartet – America, Europe, Russia and the United Nations. It is a role he relishes, seizing the challenge of the intractable Israeli–Palestinian conflict and the opportunity to break the 60-year-old stalemate. Observers were less enthusiastic about Blair's appointment, seeing him as a tainted figure who led Britain into an unjust war and few envied him the task of unravelling the complex, multiple issues that keep the two sides apart. His reputation as a 'friend' of Israel is also thought to be unhelpful, even though his involvement in the Middle East has been far from one-sided. (For example, he continues to oppose Israel's 'separation wall' that Palestinians regard as a threat to their livelihoods.) But does Blair have a fighting chance of making a difference to an embittered and entrenched conflict that has defeated a host of world leaders before him? Cherie was quoted as saying, 'Only my husband would consider taking on one of the most dangerous, difficult jobs in the world.'

Since 2003, the Quartet has tried and failed to reach a peaceful solution in the Middle East, a mission regarded as the Holy Grail of international diplomacy. How to reassure Israel of their long-held security concerns, how to reinvigorate the Palestinian economy and 'change things on the ground' and how to reach a settlement without a mandate to negotiate with Hamas (although it is widely believed that unofficial talks have taken place). On taking up his appointment, Blair, with the backing of George Bush, pledged to work towards a settlement by 2009 that would declare a Palestinian state peacefully co-existing alongside Israel; those on the sidelines remained doubtful that any real progress could be made. Blair had limited powers to negotiate although some believed that his political stature would compensate for the modest negotiating powers at his disposal. But the director of a large Jewish-based British organization was one of a number of people who doubted the high-profile advocate. 'Blair is like a movie star. One moment he is smiling at the camera and the next moment he's gone.' Another warned that the large Muslim community took a dim view of Blair's patronage of the Christian population and hoped that Christians would not have to pay a heavy price for his support. Nevertheless, at the time of his appointment, Palestinian officials believed privately that his status as a world leader and his closeness to George Bush would pump energy into the peace process. (And Blair liked to remind the American President that the Northern Ireland Agreement was signed during his last month in office.)

Giving evidence to the House of Commons Select Committee in his role as Middle East envoy, Blair admitted that his view of the situation had changed radically since standing down as Prime Minister:

> What we need to do is get a period of calm, to get a ceasefire in Gaza, progressively to start reopening the crossings, start to get proper humanitarian help through and then build your way back out of this situation where the people of Gaza can be helped; and secondly, and very importantly, the situation in Gaza does not disrupt other possibilities in progress.[2]

Resolving the Arab–Israeli conflict, Blair believed, would be an enormous boost to the forces of moderation, a symbolic act not just between Israel and Palestine but Islam and the West. And he saw strong similarities to Northern Ireland.

> What each side says about the other is essentially true: namely, what the Palestinians say about the injustice of occupation, and what the Israelis say about the security problems. You have to deal with those realities and change things practically. You will not get a peace deal first. It has to begin on the ground with people seeing changes in their daily lives.[3]

For a while, the Middle East region was seen to be moving slowly towards a possible settlement. Jordan and Egypt presented a peace plan on behalf of the Arab people. Israel appeared willing to engage with a moderate wing of the Palestinian authorities. Blair raised more than $7 billion to invest in reconstruction to invigorate the Palestinian economy. And in May 2008, he announced a breakthrough in negotiations with Israel when Israel agreed to ease travel and trade restrictions that were damaging the Palestinian economy. 'This is a first step, but it's a significant first step. It will make a marked improvement' Blair told a news conference.[4]

At about the same time, there were pleasing announcements on two other fronts: Wataniya, a mobile-phone company, pledged to invest $700 million over ten years in Palestine creating 750 jobs and 1,500 indirect jobs, and the renovation of a sewage treatment plant in Northern Gaza – one of Blair's top priorities – was completed in June 2008 (although a visit to the site had to be postponed because of a specific security threat).

Blair insisted that these were small but essential improvements to the lives of Palestinians that would persuade them that 'things were happening on the ground' and long-standing, more complex issues would be resolved in time, with peaceful coexistence the prize trophy. The key issue was to convince Hamas that there was everything to gain from ending rocket attacks on Israel from the Gaza Strip, after which the Arab peace plan could be implemented – a two-state solution that would give the Palestinian state independence, democracy and viability that would not threaten Israeli security.

A hint of optimism hung in the air, but the Israeli attacks on

Gaza in December 2008 changed everything. The assault on the Palestinians put an end to dreams of a two-state solution. For the foreseeable future, no Palestinian leader would dare to be seen talking to those Israeli leaders who were responsible for ordering F-16s into Gaza, the same leaders who embarked on a ground offensive to curtail Hamas rocket attacks and to prevent supplies from Egypt – intended for Hamas – through the tunnels along the Gaza–Sinai border. Calls for a ceasefire from the international community would go unheeded until the eve of the inauguration of Barack Obama.

Blair remained bullish. In a BBC interview, he insisted that there was a 'basis' for an immediate ceasefire if the supply of arms into Gaza was halted. 'If we want to resolve this, we can. We have to grip it and sort it. If we do that with requisite dedication, energy and commitment, we can resolve it.' Yet he acknowledged in an interview with Haaretz: 'How do you negotiate the two-state problem with people if they don't accept your right to exist? That's the problem. Some people tell me, "You spoke with the IRA" and I tell them we only did that once they accepted that the solution will only be through peaceful means.'

The Middle East road map for peace has consumed hours of negotiations and initiatives and defeated some of the finest diplomatic brains while costing the lives of thousands of Israeli and Palestinian civilians. While titanic struggles and reassessments continue to take place within religions, the implications are profound in the struggle between reactionary Islam and mainstream Islam. Rarely have faith issues and religious extremism been so central to fanning and prolonging conflict, not just in the Middle East but around the world. Blair outlined the ultimate aim:

> The real impact of a settlement is more than correcting the plight of the Palestinians. It is that such a settlement would be living, tangible visible proof that the region and therefore the world can accommodate different faiths and cultures, even those who have been in vehement opposition to each other.[5]

While Blair is unlikely to bring total solutions to the Israeli–Palestinian conflict, tentative steps were being made towards the reconstruction of Palestine with positive results on the West Bank, although problems in Gaza were never seriously addressed. The stakes remain high and so does the level of suspicion on both sides. This means that at some stage Blair's role as peace envoy must involve looking at the broader Arab–Israeli religious question – the historic roots of their hostilities – or face the weary silence that perpetuates doubt on both sides.

Blair's commitment to the peace process remains strong, although at the time of writing, the world – and Blair – await the outcome of the Israeli election, the appointment of the US special envoy to the Middle East, Senator George Mitchell, and the political fallout of the latest attacks on Gaza. The Quartet's Special Envoy nevertheless spends one week in four in Jerusalem and the widely held belief is that the Middle East is Blair's public penance for the Iraq war, although he refuses to accept the hypothesis:

Obviously I take a different view of the war from most people but it's true that I feel a sense of responsibility for this region. I don't feel I'm putting something right because I see this all as the same basic struggle: getting rid of Saddam, the Palestinian peace process, pushing back against Iran, sorting out Lebanon, a struggle about which the western world is pretty much asleep.[6]

Blair accepts a sense of responsibility but will never accept that he is on a mission to make good for past sins because he continues to believe 'I did what I believed was right.' Establishing the Tony Blair Inter-Faith Foundation in May 2008 became a conduit for 'what he believes is right' and the peace plan for the Middle East is the template, bringing together faiths and cultures and working together peacefully, to rid Islam, Judaism and Christianity of extremism, bigotry and hatred. Blair continues to remind any audience willing to listen that religion, rather than secular politics, is the power base for the future, that politics is no longer about left and right but about closed and open, and inter-faith activity keeps minds open just as extremism shuts them down. The world looks on quizzically, knowing that to object to such a commendable initiative would be like rubbishing mother's apple pie, Mother Teresa and the state of grace. No one can accuse Blair of lacking ambition, although the scale of the vision, vying with what is achievable, might thwart the outcome.

So what is the Foundation? It is not about 'chucking faith into a doctrinal melting pot', says Blair, but about living, learning about and working with people of different faiths, rescuing religion from extremism. It focuses on the three Abrahamic religions as well as Hinduism, Sikhism and Buddhism, and has four specific aims: furthering the Millennium Development Goals (the litmus test of world values) with its first task of working towards ending the scourge of malaria and eradicating the disease in five to ten years; establishing a new course at Yale University – 'Faith and Globalization' – to educate on inter-faith matters, with Blair leading a series of seminars every year; establishing Abraham House in London, a standing exhibition, library and convention centre for inter-faith work; and supporting organizations which strive to counter extremism and promote reconciliation in matters of religious faith. Deliberately steering clear of doctrinal disputes, the intention is to refrain from imposing judgements in the name of the Foundation, creating a moderate voice of all faiths, a voice that exudes mutual respect and a regard for others.

Blair's lecture at Westminster Cathedral on 'Faith and Globalization' set out the detail of the Foundation's work. But first he addressed the question of why religion was important in his life, why faith was good in itself and how God had been an essential prop in his public life. Faith and politics were generally regarded as ill-suited bedfellows, he said, because politicians who 'do God' are seen as 'weird', 'pretending to be better than the next person'. There was also a 'packet of trouble' showered by the media on politicians who dared discuss their religious beliefs openly:

I am not a religious leader. Actually today I am no longer a political leader. I am aware of all the jibes and ridicule that attends anyone in politics speaking about religion. I make no claims to moral superiority. Quite the opposite. But I am passionate about the importance of faith to our modern world and about the need for people of faith to reach out to one another. I can't prove that religious faith offers something more than humanism. But I believe profoundly that it does. And since religious faith has such a strong, historical and cultural influence on both East and West, it can help unify around common values what otherwise might be a battle for domination.[7]

In explaining the work of the Foundation, he showed the passion that he had once displayed as leader of the Labour Party, producing specific targets (one million bed nets for malaria sufferers, top quality research material to be displayed in Abraham House) and quantifying the benefits wherever possible, a familiar Blair trademark that says our plans are doable and here are the facts that will persuade the world. Unabashed at expressing his personal faith, the Westminster audience heard him identify it as 'rediscovering our essential humility before God, our dignity as found in our lives being placed at the service of the Source and Goal of everything'. It was Elmer Gantry, Jesuitical, a former Prime Minister unshackled, staking his claim as a leader of faith communities, completing a circular journey that began 35 years earlier in a room at St John's College, with Peter Thomson.

One surprising omission in the Foundation's first manifesto, with its emphasis on values and interdependence, is the question of human rights. It may be that in addressing human rights, Blair would tread on the toes of too many world leaders for little gain, or that human rights issues are too political for the Foundation's limited remit or it remains a target for the future, but the gaping hole remains curious.

Blair launched the Foundation at the Time Warner Center in New York, using the language of a man of the cloth and the tools of the pollster. Why the Foundation? Armed with the latest Gallup Poll information on religious attitudes, Blair told his audience that the poll showed that most Christians want better relations between Christianity and Islam, but believe that most Muslims do not. Most Muslims want better relations but believe that most Christians do not. Most Americans think most Muslims do not accept other religions while most Muslims said they wanted more, not less interaction between religions.

> So religion matters. And there is a lot of fear around between faiths. In summary, you cannot understand the modern world unless you understand the importance of religious faith. Faith motivates, galvanizes, organizes and integrates millions upon millions of people. Here is the crucial point. Globalization is pushing people together. Interdependence is reality. Peaceful co-existence is essential. If faith becomes a countervailing force, pulling people apart, it becomes destructive and dangerous. If it becomes an instrument of peaceful co-existence, reaching out to people, to treat diversity as a strength, then Faith becomes

an important part of making the twenty-first century work.[8]

He went on to suggest that his work may sound impossibly idealistic, and heads nodded in agreement but, he repeated, it was the only way to organize our affairs, adding implausibly, 'Indeed idealism becomes the new realism.' The politician, with the glib phrase to hand, is never far away, scolded one political commentator.

For the former Prime Minister, who was careful to keep his faith below the radar while in office, the tone of the lecture, despite his protests to the contrary, was that of a religious leader, words delivered with the force of his personal conviction, using the most churchy language. And there were tiny reminders of his first serious religious outings when late-night debates on faith in action made such a lasting impression on the young student. Rescuing religion from extremism and irrelevance, Blair identified his religion by and through its impact on the world rather than any personal relationship with God. If people of different faiths could co-exist happily, so could the world, 'then we can live with a sense of purpose beyond ourselves alone, supporting humanity on its journey to fulfilment'.

The congregation at Westminster Cathedral and the Times Warner audience in New York noted the content and tone of both speeches, the freelance Tony Blair liberated from the constraints of public office. But secular Britain recoiled and winced at his high moral tone, contrasting his words and missionary zeal with a war-mongering Prime Minister who had cast aside the advice of senior religious leaders when, with one voice, they had urged him to stay out of Iraq. Against the advice and pleadings of such an august body of leaders, how could he believe that God was on his side? 'There is no doubt', wrote Matthew d'Ancona, 'that he seeks authorization for war, as well as personal spiritual solace, in the Gospels.'[9]

Blair was treading a well-worn track alongside politicians throughout the ages who greased the path to war by declaring that their wars were 'just'. From the time of the French Revolution, battles were increasingly fought over moral issues or human rights that served as a smokescreen, when religion turned the military from armies, whose purpose was achieving territorial goals, to soldiers crusading for liberal democracy and ridding the world of demonized enemies. Into that same arena charged Tony Blair, a champion for justice and tolerance, challenging the enemies of freedom, offering a blueprint for liberal democracy that he felt morally bound to export.

The tragedy is that the main platform of his foreign policy – liberal interventionism – that triumphed in Kosovo and Sierra Leone, stumbled in Iraq, fatally wounding the cause. Britain is unlikely to deploy pre-emptive military strikes against corrupt government for decades to come. Yet in the war against terror, Blair believed moralists and realists were partners not antagonists, that there was no point in doing the job of Prime Minister if he was prevented from doing what he believed was right. And in the words of Peter Thomson, 'the fact that we can't solve everything doesn't mean we try to solve nothing'.[10]

JB: *What we know for certain is that if it wasn't for Tony's determination to intervene in Kosovo when he could, then thousands of people would still be living in refugee camps – or worse – rather than living in their own homes. OK, life isn't perfect for them, there are still uncertainties, but there's no longer an ethical cleansing policy on the scale of 1999, and there's no longer a Milosevic. Same in Sierra Leone where the rebel forces were put down as the Taliban were in 2001. But people sadly forget these campaigns. Of course Iraq was difficult, and still is. No sane person would want to see the horrors and the chaos continuing, and it's no use pretending it's all been a great success. On the other hand, who would want to see the return of the bad old days of Saddam and his two sons – certainly not the people of Iraq. The solution now lies with the politicians, not the military, and that has to mean progress.*

I think the world expected too much too soon after the invasion, and Tony privately agrees with that – although if he says so publicly it sounds as though he's being complacent. Take Northern Ireland as an example. British forces were there for more than 30 years before a peace formula was agreed, and arguably the situation is much more complex in Iraq. I wonder what people will be saying about Iraq in 30 years' time – it needs that period of time and more to make any meaningful judgements and to make people want to live in peace. Yet just because the problems are complex, it's no reason not to look to the future. 'You have to keep trying', to quote the boss.

There's also the question of what Tony likes to call enlightened self-interest. If the West fails to intervene when it has the power to intervene, we would certainly have to face an even greater problem in the years ahead. When countries break up and anarchy reigns, we can't just walk away and pretend it isn't happening, neither can we protect Britain from terrorist attacks with improved border controls, for example. It isn't enough anymore.

Since Blair left office, political commentators who once berated him for his aggressive foreign policy have come to question Britain's current stand-off on the world stage. In August 2008, as the strength of Russia's determination to crush Georgia became apparent, Michael Portillo decried Britain's lack of leadership and visibility during the crisis. Portillo wrote that Blair would somehow have ignored the fact that France held the presidency of the European Union and would have discovered a role for himself and his country. Blair's detractors, on the other hand, say that was precisely his problem. The former Tory minister added wistfully, 'The Iraq war became unpopular but Blair's conduct of it left us in no doubt that he was a leader. He knew what he wanted and stuck to it courageously.'

During a visit to the United Nations in April 2008, Pope Benedict XVI addressed the United Nations, attacking UN members and sovereign states for their 'indifference to intervene', coming as close as diplomatically possible to directly condemning the principle of non-interference in other countries' internal affairs. His criticism of self-serving vetoes by permanent members of the UN Security Council was thinly veiled:

When presented purely in terms of legality, rights risk becoming weak positions divorced from the ethical and rational dimension which is their foundation and goal.

The Universal Declaration, rather, has reinforced the conviction that respect for human rights is principally rooted in unchanging justice, on which the binding force of international proclamations is also based. This aspect is often overlooked when the attempt is made to deprive rights of their true function in the name of a narrowly utilitarian perspective. But if faith is the bedrock of organized religion, it is less reliable as a basis for UN diplomacy.[11]

Since the 1970s, liberal voices have demanded direct action to countermand the ineffectiveness of international law and UN peacekeeping efforts: the Blair–Bush principle of pre-emptive strikes, set out in the doctrine of international community, was their response. Ironically their bullish stance has resulted in blanket non-interventionism, regardless of the compelling argument for action. Any further entanglements could hardly be less welcome in Washington or London. What business is it of ours, they ask, if people are abused and oppressed in countries beyond our shores? The pendulum has swung swiftly in their direction. Lord Ashdown, the former Liberal leader, admitted that intervention is a blunt instrument whose outcomes are not always predictable. But he warned: 'All that expenditure and pain will be less than the cost of the war that was avoided or the price of chaos which would have ensued if the international community had stayed at home.'[12]

Zimbabwe? Darfur? Tibet? There is a red-faced, sluggish silence currently, compounded by the uncertainties of the new American administration and an international community unwilling to put itself in the firing line, no matter how ethically and militarily powerful is the case for intervention.

No longer in a position to pursue the doctrine of the international community, it seems likely that Blair will take the faith-based approach of the Foundation to another level, by interceding on matters of moral and ethical principle now that he can no longer intervene on foreign soil. A former adviser to the Foundation agrees: 'Precisely because of Iraq, it will be all too easy to delegitimize intervention. He will be consciously trying to rehabilitate his version of a liberal foreign policy.'[13]

Wherever he finds an audience, Blair will continue using his finely tuned powers of persuasion to seek influence in the world through his work in the Middle East and the Foundation, and will continue to be condemned as much for his religious beliefs as his politics: on the one hand for refusing to take the tough moral decisions that Christianity demands, or using religion as a means of winning support. In his own words, Tony Blair tells it as it is – and is not:

> You don't put a hotline up to God and get the answers. The worst thing in politics is when you're so scared of losing support that you don't do what you think is the right thing. What faith can do is, not tell you what is right, but give you the strength to do it.[14]

*   *   *

Tony Blair's spiritual and political journey began in Oxford in 1972, stopping off at Number 10, and ending in Rome 35 years later. It says much about Blair's political journey that his allegiance to Rome was put on hold for the duration of his parliamentary career because, as Vatican watchers continued to caution, a Catholic prime minister might feel obliged to take orders from the Vatican rather than Parliament. If conflict arose on moral or ethical grounds, the fear might be that the Pope would impose his will on the British parliamentary system and, as the *ingenioso* Don Quixote noted, 'fear has many eyes and can see underground'.

The constitution continues to bar Catholics from marrying a sovereign or becoming sovereign themselves, and although there is no constitutional reason to explain it, Britain has never had a Catholic prime minister. Not surprisingly, Blair's strong religious leaning to the Catholic Church was always regarded with alarm by the largely secular press and political advisers. 'Would popery return to stalk the corridors of power?' they whispered in corners. Nor was there elation from the Catholic lobby who believed that Blair was the most anti-Catholic politician for decades, with a voting record on family and moral issues that was nothing short of abysmal. This was the classic 'Rome versus Home' debate that has dogged Catholic politicians for centuries.

The British, unlike the Americans, have long been suspicious of any public declaration of faith by political leaders. George Weigel, a Catholic theologian at the Ethics and Public Policy Center in Washington, attributes Britain's unease with religion to 'the false idea that most of Europe's darkest moments can be blamed on excessive religious faith and in order to be a modern, tolerant and civil society, one has to be outside the flow of Christian history'.[15] As a result, he said, religious commitment in Britain is viewed as a kind of hobby, like keeping parakeets or breeding corgi dogs – definitely something that should not take place at the table of public conversation. Blair put it more succinctly when, in a television interview, he said that he had struggled to keep his religious views under wraps because he did not want to be perceived as a 'nutter'. In the event, it was expedient to set aside his enthusiasm for Rome that would only give rise to a bout of hysterical questions. Why else would a prime minister refuse to confront prejudice against Catholicism, a religion of five million people, by declaring his faith? Why else would he spend his entire premiership denying what was an important part of his life?

It was an undoubted quandary for an Anglican prime minister, contemplating converting to Roman Catholicism, mid-premiership. Had he been a fully paid-up member of the Catholic Church while in office, could he have voted in favour of stem-cell research, abortion, same-sex unions? Could Blair have gone to war in Iraq if he had been a Catholic? Would he not have been obliged to obey the Pope, who strongly opposed the war? And what of negotiations in Northern Ireland?

Father Caden spent many hours with Blair discussing the 'Rome versus Home' issues.

He always said, and it became even more obvious when he became prime minister, that he didn't have a right to legislate against someone else's conscience. For example, even though he was personally against abortion, legislating was something else again, and he believed that politicians should never use their own ethical views to obstruct action or change. It was never going to be a popular view, but there it is.[16]

The question of a politician's right to legislate for society, rather than blindly accepting church dogma, is hardly new. Most politicians would say that they follow their consciences: is the misfortune of an unwanted pregnancy, for example, best resolved by the trauma of termination? Precedents exist, and Catholic politicians, in raising concerns about controversial legislation on moral issues, do not have to follow Vatican diktats. More than a century ago, Cardinal Newman explained to Gladstone his position on the question of the morality of war:

> Were I actually a soldier or a sailor in Her Majesty's Service and sent to take part in a war which I could not in all conscience see to be unjust, and should the Pope suddenly bid all Catholic soldiers and sailors to retire from the service, here again taking the advice of others as best I could, I should not obey him.[17]

This from England's most celebrated convert to Catholicism who held that, apart from what he called 'interior conviction', there was no cogent proof of the existence of God and concluded in Tract 85: 'The man who has not this interior conviction has no choice but to remain agnostic while the man who has it is bound, sooner or later, to become a

Catholic.' Newman was known to have serious reservations about the declaration of papal infallibility and, in an increasingly cynical society, admitted 'Anything goes.' 'There is no positive truth in religion; one creed is as good as another; all are to be tolerated for all are matters of opinion. Rather it is the right of each individual to make religion say just what strikes his fancy.'[18] When he visited Pope Benedict in the final weeks in office, Blair took with him a signed photograph of Newman. The gift was seen as the clearest indication yet that he would be received into the Catholic Church.

JB: *Journalists have been asking me for years whether I thought Tony would become a Catholic. And I always said to them what he said to me, 'I'm happy as I am', although perhaps he should have added, 'for now'.*

There have been many occasions when I've sat in a Catholic church with Tony and the family. It was always a slightly uncomfortable moment when the family would go for Communion and Tony was left behind in the pew. I remember being at Mass at Great Missenden, sitting next to Euan. When it came to Communion, Euan whispered, 'Go on John . . . you first.' So I led the family to Communion. I'm not a Catholic but it didn't matter because no one knew who I was. But not Tony. He could only sit there excluded from something that was very important to him. It should have been Tony leading the family, not me, and that happened week after week. So I always knew that if he did convert, it would be for the sake of the family rather than for theological reasons.

But there was no way he could have converted while still Prime Minister. Constitutionally it was OK, but there were other considerations. It could have made it difficult in his relationship with the Queen. Would he have been able to appoint bishops to the Church of England? And of course it would have been positively damaging during negotiations in Northern Ireland. It might have been tricky.

Although he's able to attend Mass with the family now, and that's right, I still can't see how he can have changed his views completely. I can't imagine he's bound totally by Catholic doctrine, and obviously disagrees with some of it. For example, we spoke frequently about abortion and although he didn't believe abortion should be used as contraception, he always voted against the pro-life lobby. Same with homosexuality and same-sex marriage. And you can't suddenly change your mind on these issues although he's had to reconcile himself to some of them. Again the Vatican believes that all life is sacred and opposes birth control even in Africa where AIDS is rife. How can he suddenly start believing in that? Tony was always High Anglican anyway, so he didn't have far to go; but questions of transubstantiation, infallibility – they're difficult.

Blair's only public squabble with the Catholic Church was when Cardinal Hume was forced to intervene to stop him receiving Communion. The row rumbled on, but according to Father Caden, all was not as it seemed:

The occasion was Kathryn's First Communion at St Joan of Arc's Church in Islington. Tony told me afterwards that he hadn't planned to receive Communion but had this overwhelming feeling that he wanted to be part of the occasion, particularly because at the time they thought Kathryn would be their last child. He said he went to Communion quite impulsively. Unfortunately for Tony, there was a staunch Conservative in the congregation who telephoned the newspapers complaining that there was one law for the Blairs and one law for the rest. The story was raked over by the press day after day, and it became impossible for Cardinal Hume who had no choice other than to warn him publicly that he shouldn't take Communion. Tony was hurt but understood, and they remained firm friends until the Cardinal's death. In fact he went to see him in hospital the day before he died and they were able to have a conversation. So Tony wasn't bitter, just saddened that a member of the congregation could go to such lengths to wreak revenge.[19]

Shortly afterwards, and still a little bruised from the Communion row, Blair met a Roman Catholic priest in Liverpool. He managed to raise a smile. 'If you agree to give me Holy Communion, I'll make you Bishop of Liverpool', he joked. But his days of haggling for the sacrament were almost over.

Father Caden was one of a handful of people, other than family, invited to attend a Mass held at the private chapel of Cardinal Cormac Murphy-O'Connor when, in December 2007, six months after leaving office, Blair was received into the Catholic Church.

It was all kept deadly secret. I got a phone call on the Thursday telling me that Tony would be received into the Church on the Saturday and Cherie would be in touch. Of course it was a very busy time for me in the parish, being so near Christmas, but I managed to get there with about half an hour to spare. It was a very private occasion and very moving. There was the family of course, and some neighbours from Islington and myself. That was it. Mass was celebrated, and that's when Tony made his profession of faith: 'I believe and profess all that the holy Catholic Church teaches and proclaims to be revealed by God.' Then the Cardinal confirmed him. Yes, it was quite an honour to be there, a lovely family occasion. It was also a pleasure to see little Leo again, who managed to say the Hallelujahs in between the gospel. The last time I saw him, I'd baptized him.[20]

Blair's move from Anglican to Catholic was marked with respect all around. A church statement released the following day made no reference to the tensions within the Church following Blair's conversion. It said only that he had undergone, as Catholic converts do, a period of spiritual preparation. The Archbishop of Canterbury offered Blair and his family best wishes. Meanwhile the press smirked and spluttered and fed on Britain's deeply embedded mistrust of the politician at prayer. The *Sunday Mirror*'s headline screamed: 'I'm Holy Blair.' *The Sunday Times* predicted, 'Here Comes Trouble Father'. The cartoonists had their say, with the Pope in the Vatican saying to a colleague: 'I like Mr Blair but his holier-than-thou attitude is hard to take.'

The press may have regarded the episode as a harmless pastime but the hardliners spat blood. A spokesman for the Society for the Protection of Unborn Children said: 'We need to hear a full repudiation from him. Without one, having Blair as a Catholic is like having a vegetarian in a meat-eating club. It simply does not make sense.'[21] Anne Widdecombe, a recent convert and Tory maverick, reinforced the worst possible anti-Catholic stereotype, capturing the headlines by demanding that Blair should have been made to publicly confess his sin of refusing to outlaw abortion.

Father Caden shook his head sadly at the outburst.

> Yes, of course he was at odds with the Church on some issues, but should it have gone against him becoming a Catholic? Of course not. When people suggest otherwise, I remind them of Jesus of Nazareth on the cross, with a sinner on each side of him, repentant; and if someone turns to God directly, truthfully and asks forgiveness, then that's the important thing. No one has the right to demand that Tony Blair or anyone else makes a public recantation, as suggested by the Society for the Protection of the Unborn Child and others. Why should it be public?[22]

Yet Blair's conversion looks curious when glancing over his shoulder at those mentors who were the inspiration for his political stance and worldview; most disavowed orthodox religion, uneasy with the strict teachings of the Catholic Church. In no particular order, Blair admits that he has been strongly influenced by Hans Küng, the radical Catholic theologian, a dissident Catholic, who continues to question the Church's teaching on, for example, papal infallibility (which he believes is man-made and therefore reversible); and in relation to the authority of the Church, he says that 'there can be no absolute standpoint'. Küng's thinking has echoes of John Macmurray, a major influence on Blair during his early political and spiritual life, who concluded that religion was about community, fellowship and friendship, and refused to be a member of any church. And most influential of all was the Australian Anglican priest Peter Thomson, who operated well outside conventional churchgoing. (Thomson's son, Christian, said of Peter, 'Dad was never a priest who walked about in a cloak. He said you don't have to be in a church to be a good person'.)[23] And surprisingly in his Westminster Cathedral lecture, Blair chose to quote only one religious figure, Karen Armstrong, an ex-nun and writer who has been a regular critic of the Catholic faith. It was a curious choice and begged the question: why not choose a Catholic speaker to quote at a Catholic-sponsored event only months after converting to the Catholic Church? Armstrong is no supporter of the idea of 'the one true Church'. 'I can't see any one of them as having the monopoly of truth, any one of them as superior to any of the others. All the great traditions are, in my view, saying the same thing in much the same way, despite their surface differences.'[24]

So the chorus of Blair's mentors, with their near homogenous thinking on orthodox religion, sits strangely alongside his decision to convert to one of the most authoritarian of the Christian religions that is itself facing pressure for reform and refuting it. The exception is Cherie Blair, who never doubted that her husband would convert when the moment was right, drawn to the 'certainties and liturgies of Catholicism'. So will the former Prime Minister, who has always described himself as a 'liberal Christian', appear comfortable in papal colours?

Cardinal Newman, who continued searching for the truth of his God, noted on the occasion of his conversion: 'I was not conscious of a former faith in the fundamental truths of revelation or of more self-command; I had not more fervour; but it was like coming into port after a rough sea and my happiness on that score remains to this day without interruption.'[25]

'Coming into port after a rough sea' might well describe Tony Blair's long journey to Rome after years of negotiating the tricky waters of religious conviction alongside legislative demands and responsibilities. In practical terms, he can share Communion with his wife and children without incurring the wrath of priests, but it is difficult to imagine how he can reconcile membership of the Catholic Church with his old 'liberal Christianity'.

Perhaps the conundrum can only be seen as part of a bigger picture because, for all that has been written about him, Blair remains a mystery. Loved and loathed in equal measure. Agreeable, eager to please, sometimes hapless. In his early days as Prime Minister, regarded as the master of rhetoric with little substance; in latter years ruthless and steely. A firm leader that the Labour Party is learning to do without. A leader that people were more likely to spurn when he bared his soul, when he declared his pain and anguish for the poor and dis-possessed, for Africa, 'a scar on the conscience of the world'. Blair divided public opinion at home like no other political leader in recent times, for, despite his repeated justification for his aggressive foreign policy, anti-war protestors can see no good reason to shed blood in battles that were not their concern. Maybe *Private Eye* captured the spirit of the man, casting him as the ambitious Vicar of St Albion, Tony Blair who turned doing good into a political and personal mission.

To give credit, he went some way in accepting that mistakes were made but never wavered in his belief that, if a country could act, it must do so, challenging oppression, poverty, dictators, and if necessary by force because 'it was the right thing to do'. However, to those with moderate tendencies, Blair's ethical policy was less irrefutable, the moderates who struggled to find a middle way and struggled, moreover, to determine which side the angels were on.

JB: *As I said right at the start of this project, I could never be totally objective about Tony, which doesn't mean that I haven't been critical over the years – of course I have. But his critics have had a field day, so perhaps it's time to balance the books. And how do I see it, looking back?*

It seems a lifetime ago that Tony came to Sedgefield and I watched him then, a bit of a greenhorn, slowly growing into a leader, then Prime Minister, who remodelled the Party at a time when its future was in doubt. We were going nowhere. Kinnock and Smith set the ball rolling, but Tony went further than either of them. There were many in the Labour Party who didn't always like

---

what he was doing, but they were grateful come election time when even some of the MPs in marginal seats managed to hang on in there.

I've listened to critics and the malcontents and the foul-mouthed having a go at him, and I've sometimes actually found it hurtful on his behalf. This was a man, who could have made a very good living as a barrister, who gave it up because he wanted to change the world for the better. But then you're going to ask, how do you square that with what he did as leader of the Party, Prime Minister, world leader? How do you square his foreign policy ambitions with his Christian faith? How do you square becoming a Catholic with his voting record in the House of Commons?

What he proved throughout is that he's his own man. Some see it as pride, self-importance, and there is a sense of him believing that 'he knows best'. But being a leader is precisely that – not dithering, taking the initiative and consulting with others of course. There is a view, expressed in this book too, that his religious beliefs made him so sure of himself that he didn't always listen to advice; that too is correct, but it's all part of leading from the front. You can only listen for so long, then decisions have to be made. 'He knew what he wanted and stuck to it courageously. Like Margaret Thatcher before him, he made it impossible for any opposition leader to compete.'[26] Not the view of the Labour Party but Michael Portillo.

I've spent hours and hours in his company – in the back of cars on the way to events, in formal meetings and over a pint at the Red Lion. I truly believe that his Christianity affected his policy-making on just about everything from aid to Africa, education, poverty, world debt and intervening in other countries when he thought it was right to do it. And what I know for certain is that life would have been much more comfortable for him if he hadn't insisted on sticking to his principles. This was a Prime Minister who, for most of his time in office, led a government with a strong economic record, who made a difference in schools and hospitals, introduced the minimum wage, negotiated peace in Northern Ireland. He didn't have to challenge Clinton over Kosovo. He didn't need to get alongside the Americans after 9/11 to prove himself. More than that – he knew he was putting his job on the line, especially over Iraq. But the fervour was part of him and it comes back to it being Christian fervour that spurred him into action for better or worse, and continues now in the Middle East and the Faith Foundation. There are those who say again that he uses religion to win votes. It doesn't work like that in this country – quite the reverse. There was never going to be any political gain in making his religious beliefs known, not in a country that shies away from religion.

But the press will always find something to have a go at. Another target since he left office is paid work; Blair making hundreds of thousands of pounds from giving lectures and as adviser to banks and the like. And he does make a lot of money. But what people don't know is that it takes millions of pounds a year to run his office. He has 70 staff worldwide, an office complex in the centre of London to run both Foundations, his work in the Middle East, climate change and whatever else. It's a huge responsibility funding it all. Having said that, he is spreading himself thinly; but you can't change him – not even Cherie who sees less of him now than she did when he was Prime Minister.

I also think back to the time when he was just a young married man who went on to become a father of four, and a caring father at that. If the children ever did anything wrong, he would never smack their backsides as I might have done with mine, but he'd take them to one side and talk to them, reason with them – and yes, he has four great kids. And you know, there's the reason why he finally became a Catholic – to be with them at church and at Communion. Without the family, I reckon he would have carried on as he was – a High Anglican churchgoer who wasn't far removed from the Catholic Church anyway.

If it all sounds as though the past 25 years have been blood, sweat and tears, that's not the case. You know, when you're going around the constituency with the Prime Minister by your side, everyone is always on their best behaviour. And sometimes they bring a bit of light relief, people not sure how to react, sometimes saying and doing the daftest things. Then sometimes there are those who sort of forgot that Tony was Prime Minister . . .

CHAPTER 10

And Finally . . .

JB: *One occasion, when Tony had been travelling quite a lot, he said he hadn't been to church for a couple of weeks, and was there a service on anywhere nearby? It was a Friday afternoon. Of course not . . . not even for a Prime Minister. Then I remembered there was one in the next village – in the chapel at Deaf Hill's Old People's Home. There wasn't time to tell the vicar, but off we went. The service had already started so we slipped in the back. After a little while, one of the old fellas who had known me for years and my father before me, turned round and dug his pal in the ribs. 'Look who's there', he said, and his pal glanced back and asked, 'Why? What? Who is it?' 'It's John Burton, haven't seen him in months.' I fell about laughing but I think Tony was quite put out . . . although he managed to smile about it later.*

*   *   *

Tony had been an MP for only a year when the miners' strike started. Some people said he was more sympathetic to Thatcher than to the National Union of Mineworkers, which wasn't the case although he believed that the union was far too powerful. Nevertheless he wanted to show solidarity. Can you imagine Tony Blair on a picket line? Well, it didn't go according to plan. We went to Nottingham where there had been some heavy scenes with police and pickets battling it out. The police had blocked the exits from the motorway leading into the city centre to prevent flying pickets adding to their problems, but because he was an MP, Tony was able to get through the blockade, so off we went to support our comrades. None of us knew Nottingham, but eventually we saw the pulley wheel in the distance and drove towards it. When we got there it was eerie, peaceful as chapel on a Sunday morning. Nothing. Nobody outside the pit. All very strange. Where were the pickets and the police and the press and the chaos? Eventually a bus came along and Paul Trippet walked out into the middle of the road and stopped it. 'We're here to support the miners', he said to a bemused bus driver. The driver sniffed and asked, 'Do you know where you are?' 'We're at such and such a colliery', said Paul. 'Daft buggers, no you're not. You won't find much action here. You're at a mining museum. It's full of school kids on a day out.' So there it was . . . Tony's only attempt at picketing . . . outside a mining museum full of 12-year-olds.

*   *   *

When the Blairs were living with us it was a bit chaotic because our children were still at home and we only had three bedrooms. We managed of course, and the children would take turns sleeping on the floor. We got on well together most of the time, but Cherie wasn't always an easy person to have around. I remember the day they finally moved to 'Myrobella', which is a couple of miles away. We hired an open wagon and their bits and pieces were piled up at the back. When she got there, Cherie discovered that a Victorian lamp had disappeared. It must have had sentimental value because she went ballistic. We scoured the roads and side roads we'd taken but couldn't find it. She was determined to find it, so went back to our house, raging through drawers and cupboards as though we'd hidden it. She never did find it. I suspect somewhere in Trimdon, someone made good use of the future Prime Minister's lamp. Again, that's Cherie. But at the end of the day, she's to be admired, a woman who brought up four delightful children as well as having a successful career and all that goes with being the Prime Minister's wife. And she continues to be a good friend.

*   *   *

Tony was invited to give a lecture to the Fabian Society in Newcastle and I drove him to the venue, a hotel near Central Station. As I got out of the car I heard something rip, the back of my pants – and it wasn't just a little tear either. I'd ripped them right across the back. I didn't have an overcoat to cover my embarrassment so I said, 'Tony, you're on your own. I can't come like this.' He said, 'Of course you have to come. I'll make sure I stay close behind you.' We sidled into reception, looking like a double act, Tony close up behind me – which was fine for a while, but then we were invited to a conference room upstairs. I was paralysed at the thought of walking upstairs with nothing for cover. I spotted a gents' toilet nearby and whispered that I was going to see how bad the damage was . . . Tony followed. There he was, examining my rear end, making reassuring noises, and I got a fit of the giggles. When I finally recovered I said 'Just think what the press would make of this . . . two men in a gents' toilet, one is Tony Blair. You do know that there are a couple of press photographers around for the lecture . . . just think if one walked in now. We'd be on every front page in the country.' He howled laughing, but my God, he got out fast. I spent the rest of the meeting in the back row, was relieved when he refused a coffee at the end of the lecture, and couldn't get away quick enough.

*   *   *

Strange how Sedgefield became a recognizable worldwide name. It always surprised me when it happened. I remember one day a local businessman who owns a steel erection company and had been on the council rang me. 'Can I come and see you?' 'How about next Tuesday?' I suggested. 'I need to see you now.' He arrived ten minutes later.

He was pitching work in Libya and had flown in to finalize a deal. When he arrived at the airport, suddenly he was whisked off in a big black limo to the president's palace. Poor Gareth thought he was being arrested. Anyway palace officials knew he was from Sedgefield and it was at the time when Gaddafi was trying to make amends. The UK had broken off diplomatic relations with Libya after the shooting of WPC Yvonne Fletcher and the Lockerbie disaster. At the palace, Gareth was introduced to a Ugandan friend of Gaddafi who wanted to come to Sedgefield and see me. Could he arrange it? Well, he did and I saw the Ugandan bloke who told me what Gaddafi wanted. I rang Tony who said Gaddafi probably wanted to avoid going through the embassy in London.

A few months later, Tony finally arrived at the famous Gaddafi tent in the desert, and through interpreters the meeting got under way. Suddenly Gaddafi stopped and said, 'One thing I've been wondering, Tony, why did you want camels? Why did you ask for them? Believe it or not we don't have camels here, in fact we've had to import them for you.' Tony was gobsmacked. 'Camels? I didn't ask for camels.' Then he caught the eye of the PR person and it all fell into place. Sand, desert, camels – the ingredients of a good PR picture. The PR guy got his picture, but what amazed Tony was that Gaddafi had gone to the bother of importing them. Can you imagine the reaction of the press, Tony returning with three or four camels to Downing Street? I suppose the kids might have liked the idea of having a pet camel in the Downing Street garden.

*   *   *

And finally . . .

Back to church. Tony was planning to be in the constituency one Good Friday. I told him that there was an ecumenical service, a Procession of the Cross, from the Anglican church to the Roman Catholic church, and would he like to take part? Of course he said yes. On the day of the procession they sent a new PR man from Glasgow to look after him. This guy's main concern was that the press photographers might get pictures of Tony with the cross either in front or behind him . . . something to be avoided at all costs in Alastair's world of 'We don't do God.' What could the PR guy do?

225

I told him that the procession could get under way and I'd wait with Tony and we'd follow at the back, with the cross, naturally, leading at the front. Problem solved, you might think. Then this bright spark, still nervous of his task of looking after the Prime Minister, had a brainwave and uttered the immortal words: 'Couldn't we have the procession without the cross?'

I looked at him to see if he was winding me up. I said slowly, very slowly . . . 'It's the whole point. A procession. And a cross . . . which is why it's called the Procession of the Cross.' Where do they get them from? But it says it all really. If they couldn't understand the point of the procession, how were they ever going to understand Tony? How would they ever understand what the Prime Minister was all about?

Notes

St John's College, Oxford, 1972–5
1. *Daily Mail*, 27 January 1996.
2. *Newsnight*, BBC 2, 10 June 1994.

Introduction
1. Tony Blair, interview on *Today*, BBC Radio 4, 2 February 2007.
2. Keith Proud, *The Grit in the Oyster*, The Northern Echo, 2003.
3. Private interview.

Chapter 1
1. Tony Blair, *Sunday Telegraph*, Easter Sunday 1996.
2. Martyn Harris, *Sunday Telegraph*, 18 March 1990.
3. *The Sunday Times*, 17 July 1994.
4. Peter Thomson, interview on *Keys of the Kingdom*, Australian TV, 29 June 2000.
5. John Macmurray, *Reason and Emotion*, Prometheus Books, 1999, p. 98.
6. John Macmurray, *Conditions of Freedom,* Prometheus Books, 1993.
7. Sarah Hale, *Blair's Community*, Manchester University Press, 2006, Introduction.
8. *New Statesman*, 13 July 1994.
9. Anthony Seldon, Peter Snowdon and Daniel Collings, *Blair Unbound*, Simon and Schuster, 2007, Introduction.
10. Polly Toynbee, *Guardian*, 28 March 2001.
11. ThirdWay interview with Blair, 14 September 1993.
12. Tony Blair's letter to Michael Foot, July 1982.

Chapter 2
1. Anthony Seldon, *Blair: The Biography*, Free Press, 2004.
2. Proud, *The Grit in the Oyster*, Tony Blair Foreword.
3. Lily Burton, private interview, August 2008.
4. Fr John Caden, private interview, August 2008.

Chapter 3

1. Leslie Smith, *Harold Wilson: The Authentic Portrait*, Hodder & Stoughton, 1964.
2. Stephen Byers, in conversation, August 2008.
3. Tony Blair's Maiden Speech, 6 July 1983.
4. John Macmurray, *Freedom in the Modern World*, Prometheus Books, 2004, p. 215.
5. Fr John Caden, private interview, August 2008.
6. Philip Stephens, *Tony Blair: The Making of a World Leader*, Viking, 2004, p. 19.
7. Seldon, *Blair: The Biography*.
8. Tony Blair's Press Conference, 10 April 1992.
9. Tony Blair, Labour Party Conference, 1992.
10. Richard Dawkins, *The God Delusion*, Bantam Books, 2006, p. 342.
11. Speech to the Wellingborough Labour Party, 19 February 1993.
12. John Rentoul, *Tony Blair: Prime Minister*, Time Warner Paperbacks, p. 195.

Chapter 4

1. Labour Party Conference, 1995.
2. Fabian Society pamphlet, September 1998.
3. Seldon, *Blair: The Biography*, p. 135.
4. Anthony Giddens, *Where Now for New Labour?*, Polity Press, 2002.
5. Alastair Campbell, *The Blair Years: The Alastair Campbell Diaries*, Hutchinson, 2007, entry for 6 June 2000, p. 457.
6. Anthony Seldon quoting Matthew d'Ancona interview, April 1996, p. 519.
7. Campbell, *The Blair Years: The Alastair Campbell Diaries*, entry for 6 April 1996.
8. Tübingen University speech, 'Value and Community', 30 June 2000.
9. Tony Benn, website, www.tonybenn.com.
10. Tony Blair to Matthew d'Ancona, 6 April 1996.
11. Fernando Henrique Cardosa, *The Accidental President of Brazil*, Public-Affairs US, 2006.
12. Fr John Caden, private interview, August 2008.
13. Tony Blair, pre-election briefing, May 1997.

Chapter 5

1. David Remnick, *The Observer*, 1 May 2005.
2. Dawkins, *The God Delusion*, p. 259.
3. National Secular Society, website, www.secularism.org.uk.
4. 'Scars On My Back' speech, British Venture Capital Association Conference, 6 July 1999.
5. Graham Dale, *The Observer*, November 1998.
6. Polly Toynbee, *Guardian*, April 1999.

7. Giddens, *Where Now for New Labour?*
8. Stephens, *Tony Blair: The Making of a World Leader*, p. 89.
9. Seldon, *Blair: The Biography*, p. 135.
10. Blair's Millennium Speech, Trimdon Colliery Community Centre, 29 December 1999.
11. Peter Thomson: TV interview on 'Keys of the Kingdom', Australian TV, January 2000.
12. Nick Davies, *Flat Earth News*, Chatto & Windus, 2008.
13. Following the 2001 election result, 8 June 2001.
14. Exchange of letters between Philip Gould and Paul Thompson, editor of *Renewal*, 2 January 2003.
15. Seldon et al., *Blair Unbound*, Introduction.

Chapter 6
1. W. B. Yeats poem 'Easter 1916'.
2. Dawkins, *The God Delusion*.
3. Martin McGuinness, interview in the *Guardian*, 14 March 2007.
4. Tony Blair, interview in the *Daily Mirror*, 26 September 1996.
5. Bill Blair, interview in the *Observer*, 27 April 2003.
6. Tony Blair addressing the Irish Parliament, 26 November 1998.
7. Campbell, *The Blair Years: The Alastair Campbell Diaries*, entry for 12 May 1997.
8. Tony Blair, interview in *The Times*, 6 July 2008.
9. Tony Blair, speech to the Irish Parliament, 26 November 1998.
10. Tony Blair speech, Tübingen University, 30 June 2000.
11. Campbell, *The Blair Years: The Alastair Campbell Diaries*.
12. Ian Paisley, interview in the *Guardian*, 14 March 2007.
13. Seldon et al., *Blair Unbound*, p. 515.
14. Ian Paisley, church newsletter, March 2007.
15. Ian Paisley, Stormont, 27 March 2007.
16. Tony Blair, Stormont, 8 May 2007.
17. Tony Blair's resignation speech, Sedgefield, 10 May 2007.

Chapter 7
1. St Augustine, quoted in *The Heart is a Little to the Left*.
2. Tony Blair, speech to Chicago Economic Club, 22 April 1999.
3. Tony Blair, speech to Cape Town Parliament, January 1999.
4. John F. Kennedy, Berlin, 26 June 1963.
5. Tony Blair, House of Commons, 23 March 1999.
6. Tony Blair, House of Commons, 23 March 1999.
7. Tony Blair, speech to Romanian Parliament, 4 May 1999.
8. Amitai Etzionoi, RSA Lecture, *Foreign Policy After Bush*, 4 June 2007.
9. Labour Party Conference, Brighton, 2 October 2001.

10. Pope John Paul, Italian religious TV channel, Telespace, March 2003.
11. Sir Christopher Meyer, *Observer* magazine, March 2007.
12. Tony Blair speech, Sedgefield, 5 March 2004.
13. George W. Bush, Israeli–Palestine summit, 7 October 2005.
14. Roy Jenkins, House of Lords, December 2002.
15. Tony Blair speech, Sedgefield, 5 March 2004.
16. Jonathan Powell, the *Observer*, 18 November 2007.

Chapter 8
1. Harold Macmillan, Melbourne, Australia, 17 February 1958.
2. *The Economist*, April 2001.
3. Polly Toynbee, the *Guardian*, 2 September 2008.
4. David Bell, Chief Inspector of Schools, speech to Hansard Society, 7 January 2005.
5. Cherie Blair, *Speaking for Myself: The Autobiography*, Little, Brown, 2008, p. 342.
6. Cherie Blair, *Speaking for Myself*, p. 370.
7. Seldon et al., *Blair Unbound*, p. 271.
8. Seldon et al., *Blair Unbound*, private interview, p. 277.
9. Tony Blair speech, Labour Party Conference, 2004.
10. Alan Milburn, to Labour Party colleagues.
11. Philip Gould, *The Times*, 26 June 2007.
12. Peter Riddell, *The Times*, 20 March 2007.
13. Lord Turnbull on Gordon Brown, interview in the *Financial Times*, 19 March 2007.
14. Private interview.
15. Seldon et al., *Blair Unbound*.
16. Tony Blair, resignation speech, Sedgefield, 10 May 2007.
17. Alice Miles, *The Times*, 9 May 2007.
18. Michael Portillo, *The Sunday Times*, May 2007.
19. Tim Hames, *The Times*, 19 February 2007.
20. Matthew Parris, *The Times*, 23 December 2006.

Chapter 9
1. Seamus Heaney, from *The Cure at Troy* (2002), p. 77. © Faber and Faber.
2. Tony Blair, Commons Select Committee, 5 June 2008.
3. Tony Blair, Commons Select Committee, 5 June 2008.
4. Tony Blair, News Conference, 13 May 2008.
5. Tony Blair, interview, 2 February 2008.
6. Interview, *The Sunday Times*, 6 July 2008.
7. Westminster Cathedral lecture, 3 April 2008.
8. Launch of Inter Faith Foundation, New York, 30 May 2008.
9. Peter Osborne quotes Matthew d'Ancona, *The Spectator*, 5 April 2003.

10. Thomson, 'Keys of the Kingdom'.
11. Pope Benedict XVI, United Nations, 18 April 2008.
12. Lord Ashdown, Institute for Strategic Studies, 21 February 2007.
13. Private interview, August 2008.
14. Tony Blair, *Time* magazine, 29 May 2008.
15. George Weigel, *Chicago Tribune*, 30 December 2007.
16. Fr John Caden, private interview, August 2008.
17. Cardinal Newman, letter to the Duke of Norfolk, 27 December 1874.
18. Cardinal Newman, lecture 1879, quoted in *Theologians for Beginners*, Revd Dr Gerald McDermott.
19. Fr John Caden, private interview, August 2008.
20. Fr John Caden, private interview, August 2008.
21. John Smeaton, Society of Unborn Children, 11 January 2008.
22. Fr John Caden, private interview, August 2008.
23. Christian Thomson, TV interview on 'Keys of the Kingdom', Australian TV, January 2000.
24. Karen Armstrong, the *Financial Times*, 27 August 2007.
25. Cardinal Newman's autobiography, *Apologia pro Vita Sua*, 1864/65.
26. Michael Portillo, *The Sunday Times*, 17 August 2008.